2024 IGE Distinguished Lecture Forum

2024년 미국 대선과 동북아 지정학적 리스크: 한국의 외교안보전략 시사점
미국 대선 이후 무역정책 변화와 중국 및 한국 경제에 미치는 영향 분석

초판 1쇄 발행 2024년 12월

펴낸이 전광우
지　원 김경진, 김시연
디자인 김정진
인　쇄 한진기획인쇄

펴낸곳 세계경제연구원
전　화 02-551-3334~8
팩　스 02-551-3339
등　록 서울시 강남구 영동대로 511

종이책 ISBN 979-11-6177-048-2 [03320]

종이책 정가 15,000원

*이 책은 저작권법에 따라 보호받는 저작물이므로 무단 전재와 복제를 금합니다.
*잘못된 책은 구입하신 서점에서 바꾸어 드립니다.

2024 IGE Distinguished Lecture Forum

2024년 미국 대선과 동북아 지정학적 리스크: 한국의 외교안보전략 시사점
Victor Cha

미국 대선 이후 무역정책 변화와 중국 및 한국 경제에 미치는 영향 분석
Jeffrey J. Schott

2024년 미국 대선과 동북아 지정학적 리스크: 한국의 외교안보전략 시사점

빅터 차
(Victor Cha)

빅터 차

Victor Cha

미국 외교정책 및 대외전략 분야의 국제적 권위자로 미 조지타운대학교의 부학장이자 교수로 재직 중이며, CSIS 국제전략문제연구소의 수석부소장이자 한국석좌를 맡고있다. 백악관 국가안전보장회의 아시아 디렉터, 부시 행정부 북한 특별 보좌관 등 요직을 두루 역임했다.

[2024년 4월 2일]

2024년 미국 대선과 동북아 지정학적 리스크: 한국의 외교안보전략 시사점

빅터 차
미 조지타운대학교 석좌교수
CSIS (국제전략문제연구소) 아시아 담당 부소장 및 한국석좌

전광우 이사장: 안녕하십니까? 세계경제연구원 웨비나에 오신 것을 환영합니다. 오늘은 미국의 외교정책, 특히 아시아 관련 세계적 권위자이신 빅터 차 박사님을 모시고 미국-중국 간의 긴장 상황, 북한의 도발, 그리고 최근 북한과 러시아 간의 동맹 강화 등 특히 악화되고 있는 지정학적 도전과 이에 따른 주요 외교, 안보 현안을 논의할 예정입니다. 또한, 이러한 대외환경 변화가 한국에 미치는 전략적 시사점도 모색할 예정입니다. 이 주제에 빅터 차 교수님만큼 적합한 분은 없다고 생각합니다. 오늘 차 박사님께서는 워싱턴 DC에서 직접 라이브로 접속하고 계십니다.

빅터 차 박사님께서는 현재 조지타운대학교 석좌교수로 재직 중이신데 2023년에는 조지타운 종신직 교수에게 수여되는 최고 명예인 'Distinguished University Professor'로 임명되셨습니다. 또한, 미국의 국제전략문제연구소(CSIS)에서 아시아 수석 부회장 및 한국 석좌(Senior Vice President for Asia and Korea Chair)를 맡고 계십니다. 백악관 국가안전보장회의 아시아 담당

국장을 역임하셨으며, 조지 부시 대통령 행정부에서는 대북 정책 수석 고문을 지내시기도 했습니다.

그럼 이제 소개를 마치고 빅터 차 박사님을 모시겠습니다. 약 30분간 박사님의 강연을 듣고 이후에는 토론 시간을 갖도록 하겠습니다. 차 박사님, 다시 만나 뵙게 되어 정말 기쁩니다.

빅터 차 박사: 네 감사합니다. 이사장님 다시 만나 뵙게 되어서 정말 영광입니다. 이렇게 세계경제연구원 웨비나에 참여하게 되어 매우 기쁩니다. 이사장님께서 말씀하신 것처럼 저는 먼저 한반도에서의 안보 상황에 대해 이야기하면서 시작을 해보려고 합니다. 그리고 이를 기반으로 하여 러시아와 북한의 관계, 한국에의 시사점 등에 대해 말씀드리겠습니다. 미국의 정치 상황 및 대선 전망, 이에 따른 한미 동맹 관계에의 영향에 대해서는 Q&A 시간에 다룰 예정입니다.

우선 올해 북한의 동향부터 말씀드리겠습니다. 일부에서는 전쟁이 일어날 가능성에 대해 추측하기도 했는데요, 결론부터 말씀드리자면 저도 2024년에 북한이 훨씬 더 공격적인 모습을 보일 것으로 예상하고 있습니다. 어제도 북한이 또 다시 일본 방향으로 탄도 미사일을 발사한 것으로 보도되었는데요, 올해는 이런 일이 훨씬 더 자주 일어날 것으로 예상되며, 대화의 기회는 거의 없을 것으로 보입니다. 대화가 불가능하다고 생각하지는 않지만, 현재 상황을 보면 현실적으로 이루어지기는 어려워 보입니다. 슬라이드 화면을 봐 주시기 바랍니다.

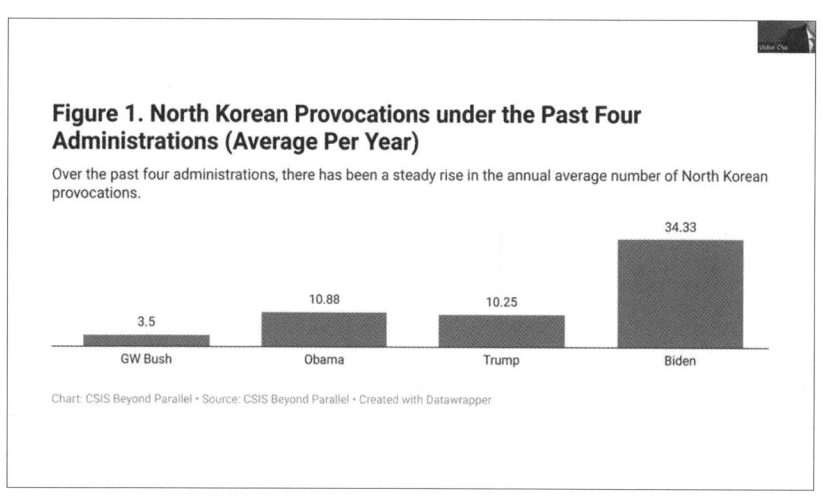

지난 네 번의 미국 대통령 임기 동안 북한의 주요 군사적 도발이 매년 평균적으로 몇 건 발생했는지를 나타내는 그래프입니다. 보시는 바와 같이 북한의 도발은 지난 몇 년 동안, 특히 지난 네 번의 미국 행정부에 걸쳐 지속적으로 증가해왔습니다. 왼쪽 끝부터 살펴보면, 조지 W. 부시 대통령 하에서는 북한의 주요 군사적 도발이 연평균 약 3.5건이었다는 것을 볼 수 있습니다. 전광우 이사장님께서 언급하신 대로, 제가 미국에서 근무했던 바로 그 행정부입니다. 그리고 이 숫자는 조금 놀라웠습니다. 왜냐하면, 실제로는 연평균 3.5건 이상으로 느껴졌기 때문입니다. 사실상 매년 3.5건이 아니라, 매달 또는 두 달에 한 번씩 도발이 일어나는 것처럼 느껴졌습니다. 그렇지만, 조지 W. 부시 대통령 하 8년 동안 북한의 주요 군사적 도발은 연평균 약 3.5건 정도였습니다.

오바마 행정부 8년을 살펴보면, 그 수치는 거의 연평균 11건에 달하는 것을 볼 수 있습니다. 아마도 아시겠지만, 오바마 행정부는 '전략적 인내(Strategic Patience)' 정책으로 잘 알려져 있습니다. 이 정책은 주로 외교보다는 북한에 대한 제재 압박을 중심으로 하여, 북한이 협상에 더 유연하게 대응할 수 있는 위치에 오도록 하려는 것이었습니다. 그래서 이 시기 동안 북한의 주요 도발은 연평균 거의 11건에 달했습니다.

이제 도널드 트럼프 대통령 하의 4년을 보면, 도발 횟수는 연평균 약 10건 정도였습니다. 이 부분은 저에게도 놀라웠습니다. 물론 트럼프 대통령 시기는 김정은과의 정상 회담 외교로 유명했지만, 그 정상 회담 외교에도 불구하고 실제로 북한의 주요 도발 횟수는 오바마 대통령 하의 8년과 큰 차이가 없었습니다. 정상 회담 외교가 없었던 오바마 행정부의 8년 동안과 거의 동일한 수치였습니다. 그리고 정말 흥미로운 점은 바이든 행정부에 접어들면서 급격한 증가가 발생한 부분입니다. 바이든 행정부 하에서는 연평균 34회의 주요 군사적 도발, 탄도 미사일 시험, 순항 미사일 시험 등과 같은 도발이 이루어졌습니다. 연평균 34건이라니, 이는 정말 엄청난 증가 추세를 의미합니다.

다음 슬라이드에서 보시면, 바이든 행정부 4년과 트럼프 행정부 4년 동안의 데이터가 연도별로 나누어져 있는데요, 슬라이드 하단을 보시면, 2017년 트럼프 행정부의 데이터를 확인하실 수 있습니다. 2017년은 '화염과 분노(fire and fury)'의 해였던 것을 기억하실 겁니다. 그 해에는 트럼프와 김정은 사이에 서로 위협하는 말을 많이 주고받았었고, 트럼프는 김정은을 "작은 로켓맨(little rocket man)"이라고 부르며 북한에 화염과 분노를 퍼붓겠다고 약속했습니다. 김정은은 트럼프를 노망이 들었다고 비난

하며, 북한은 미국의 주요 도시들을 타격할 준비가 되어 있다고 응수했습니다. 2017년은 기억하시는 바와 같이 많은 긴장과 갈등 속 매우 어려운 한 해였습니다. 상황이 통제 불능 상태로 격화될 가능성도 있었습니다.

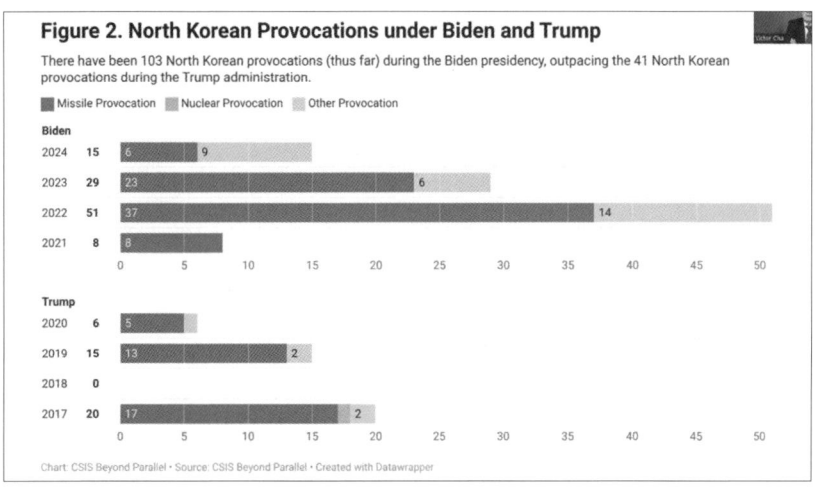

2018년을 보면, 이 해는 정상 회담이 시작된 해로, 2018년 싱가포르 정상 회담과 2019년 초에 열린 하노이 정상 회담이 있었습니다. 2018년에는 사실 북한의 도발이 전혀 없었습니다. 우리가 수집한 북한의 공격적인 행동에 대한 모든 데이터 중, 도발이 없었던 유일한 해가 바로 2018년입니다. 이는 트럼프와의 정상 회담 외교가 이루어진 해로, 북한의 공격적인 행동이 전혀 없었던 유일한 해였습니다. 그러나 우리 모두 알다시피, 2019년 2월에는 하노이 정상 회담이 실패로 끝납니다. 하노이 정상 회담에서 도널드 트럼프는 합의 없이 회담을 마무리 짓고 회담을 중단했습니다. 그 이후 북한은 다시 도발을 계속하는 방식으로 돌아갔고, 2020년까지 이러한 도발은 지속되었습니다.

이제 바이든 행정부로 넘어가면, 2021년 초에 북한은 몇 가지 도발을 했지만, 그 수가 많지는 않습니다. 저는 이것이 북한이 바이든 행정부의 대북 정책 검토 결과가 어떻게 나올지 지켜보는 단계였기 때문이라고 생각합니다. 북한은 사실상 2021년 1월 바이든 취임에서부터 2022년 1월까지, 즉 거의 1년 동안 시간을 주며 바이든 행정부가 어떤 대북 정책을 취할지 이해하려 했습니다. 그리고 마치 시계처럼, 2022년 1월이 되자 북한은 마치 스위치를 켠 듯, 전면적으로 군사적 도발을 강화하며 미사일 도발과 기타 군사적 도발을 급격히 늘렸습니다. 2022년에는 51건, 2023년에는 29건의 도발이 있었고, 2024년에는 이미 이러한 군사적 행동이 상당히 많을 것으로 예상됩니다.

데이터를 기반으로 살펴본 바와 같이, 북한의 도발 행동은 시간이 지날수록 극적으로 증가해왔다는 점을 알 수 있습니다. 그렇다면 원인이 무엇일까요? 저는 여기에 세 가지 이유가 있다고 생각합니다.

첫 번째는 미사일 발사와 시험에 관련된 과학적인 이유입니다. 현재 김정은은 다양한 종류의 미사일을 개발하고 완성하는 과정에 있습니다. 순항 미사일, 탄도 미사일 기술, 이동식 발사 미사일, 고체 연료 미사일, 탄도 미사일에 대한 대응책, 극초음속 탄두, 하나의 탄두에 여러 재진입 수단을 탑재하는 기술 등 그는 지금 다양한 기술을 개발하려고 하고 있습니다. 이를 이루기 위해서는 시험이 필요합니다. 그래서 이러한 미사일 도발이 증가하는 이유 중 하나는 바로 과학적인 개발과 실험 일정에 맞춰 이 능력들을 완성하려는 과정에 있기 때문입니다. 그렇기 때문에 더 많은 도발이 일어나고 있는 것입니다. 김정은은 미사일과 핵 개발에 대한 목표를 매우 명확하게 밝혔습니다. 그래서 이를 시험하고 데이터를 수집하며, 제대로 진행되고 있는지, 혹은 조정이 필요한지를 파악하기 위해 시험을 하고 있습니다. 컴퓨터 시뮬레이션으로 할 수 있는 일에는 한계가 있기 때문에, 실제 실험을 하는 것입니다.

또 다른 이유로는 실제 훈련과 관련이 있습니다. 제가 말씀드리고 싶은 것은, 일부 시험은 물론 과학적 개발과 관련이 있겠지만, 일부는 과학적 개발과는 상관없이 실제 실전 훈련에 집중된 부분도 있다는 것입니다. 그래서 북한이 이미 여러 차례 시험한 적이 있는 단거리 탄도 미사일이나 중거리 미사일을 계속해서 시험하는 것에 대하여, 이제 우리는 이것이 단순히 과학 개발의 문제가 아니라는 것을 생각해야 합니다. 이제 이것은 훈련의 영역으로 넘어가고 있는 것입니다.

예를 들어, 북한이 단거리 탄도 미사일을 발사하고, 그다음에 중거리 탄도 미사일 시험을 진행한 뒤, 폭격을 이어가는 이 모든 것을 종합해보면 이것은 바로 군사 훈련입니다. 즉, 실전 훈련이라는 것입니다. 이는 미국과 한국이 진행하는 군사 훈련처럼 말입니다. 북한이 단거리 및 중거리 탄도 미사일을 사용하여 장거리 타격훈련이나 핵 공격 훈련을 하고 있는 것입니다. 이것이 바로 바이든 행정부 하에 북한의 미사일 실험이 증가하는 또 하나의 이유라고 생각합니다.

그리고 이렇게 높은 빈도의 실험이 일어나는 세 번째 이유는 미국과 북한 간의 외교의 부재와 관련이 있다고 봅니다. 우리는 CSIS에서 연구를 진행했는데, 이 연구는 1990년대의 합의까지 거슬러 올라가며, 미국과 북한 간의 협상이나 외교가 진행될 때 북한의 미사일 시험, 도발적인 행동들의 빈도가 확실히 낮아진다는 상관관계를 발견했습니다. 다시 말해, 미국과 북한이 다자간 6자회담 형식이나 양자 간 협상 테이블에 앉았던 시기에는 북한의 도발이 크게 줄어들거나 없어졌다는 것입니다. 그런데 우리는 꽤 오랫동안 진지한 협상을 진행하지 못하고 있습니다. 바이든 행정부에 들어서는 사실상 어떤 협상도 없었습니다. 협상이 없었기 때문에 북한은 도발을 강화하고 있습니다. 그래서 저는 이것이 조지 W. 부시 행정부부터 오바마, 트럼프, 그리고 지금의 바이든 행정부까지 북한의 도발이 지속적으로 증가한 이유 중 하나라고 생각합니다. 이러한 해석을 바탕으로 다음 주제인 2024년 상황에 대해 다뤄보도록 하겠습니다.

저는 2024년에 북한의 군사적 시험, 도발, 훈련의 빈도가 더욱 높아질 것이라고 예상합니다. 첫 번째 이유는 바로 2024년 자체와 관련이 있습니다. 2024년은 여러분도 아시다시피 한국의 선거가 있는 해입니다. 곧 8일 후인 4월 10일에는 한국의 국회의원 선거가 있고, 11월에는 미국의 대통령 선거가 있습니다. 그리고 우리가 수집한 데이터에서는 미국 대선 시기와 북한의 도발이 많아지는 시기에는 명확한 상관관계가 있는 것으로 나타났습니다. 즉, 미국에서 대통령 선거나 의회선거가 있는 해에 북한의 활동이 훨씬 더 많아지는 경향이 있습니다.

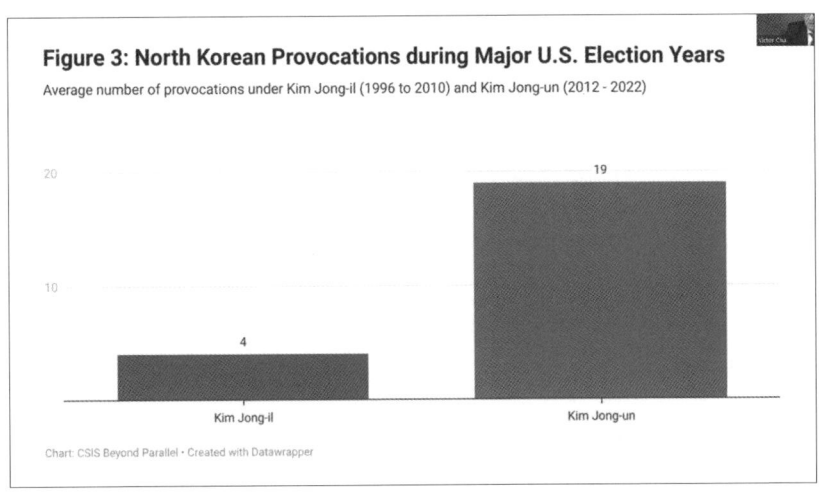

이 슬라이드는 김정일과 김정은 하에서, 미국에서 중요한 선거가 있었던 해의 북한의 도발 평균 횟수를 보여줍니다. 김정일 데이터는 1996년부터 2010년까지, 김정은 데이터는 2012년부터 2022년까지 포함됩니다. 이 데이터는 대통령 선거와 중간 선거가 모두 포함된 자료입니다. 여기 보시면, 김정은은 미국 대선이 있는 해에 김정일보다 훨씬 더 활발히 활동하는 모습을 볼 수 있고, 미국 대선과 북한의 도발 사이에도 관계가 있다는 것을 볼 수 있습니다. 저는 북한이 이러한 방식으로 2025년에 누가 미국 대통령이 되든, 그 전에 자신들의 입지를 확고히 하려는 의도를 보이고 있는 것이라 생각합니다. 도발을 강화함으로써, 북한은 자신들이 새로운 행정부에 시급한 외교 문제로 떠오르게 만들고, 이를 기회로 삼아 새 행정부가 들어오자마자 자신들이 원하는 바를 얻어내려 하는 것입니다.

제가 2024년에 북한의 도발이 증가할 것이라고 생각하는 또 다른 이유는, 올해 1, 2분기와 관련이 있습니다. 그 이유는 바로 미국의 군사 훈련 때문입니다. 미국은 현재 한국과 함께 한반도 주변에서 군사 훈련의 빈도를 높이고 있습니다. 또한, 미국, 일본, 한국 간의 새로운 삼자 훈련도 있을 예정입니다. 즉, 북한이 과거에 해왔듯이 이러한 도발에 대응해야 된다는 압박을 느끼게 될 것입니다. 특히 미국이 이러한 군사 훈련을 계속 강화함에 따라 북한의 도발 패턴이 지속될 것으로 예상됩니다.

이제 정책 측면에서 말씀드리자면, 2024년 미 군사 훈련 강화가 바이든 정부의 잘못이라고 생각하지는 않습니다. 바이든 행정부는 지난 4년 동안 북한과의 대화를 시도하기 위해 여러 방법을 통해 일관되게 노력해 왔습니다. 비공식적으로 들은 바로는, 그들이 적어도 20번 이상 북한과 접촉하려 했고, 협상 테이블로 돌아오게끔 제안했으며, 이는 핵무기, 제재 완화, 코로나 백신, 식량, 연료 등 다양한 사안에 걸쳐 있었습니다. 하지만 북한은 감감무소식이었습니다. 실제로 북한은 그 어떤 반응도 보이지 않았습니다. 북한이 미국과 대화할 의사가 없는 것은 꽤 명확해 보입니다.

이와 관련된 최근의 예시 중 하나는 아마 많은 분들이 신문에서 읽으셨을 텐데, 바로 트래비스 킹이라는 미군 병사를 북한이 송환하기로 결정한 사건입니다. 그는 한국에 주둔하던 미군 병사로, 추방 절차를 밟고 있었고, 그가 추방될 경우 아마도 군에서 불명예 제대 처분을 받았을 것입니다. 그는 인천공항에서 탈출한 뒤, DMZ로 향한 뒤 공동경비구역(JSA)을 넘어 북한으로 넘어갔습니다. 북한은 먼저 트래비스 킹 병사를 일정 기간 고립시켜 COVID 바이러스의 전파를 막으려 했습니다. 북한은 여전히

COVID 백신 인프라가 없는 나라이기 때문입니다. 그 후, 북한은 그를 몇 달 동안 심문한 뒤, 그를 다시 미국으로 송환하려고 했습니다. 이는 처음 있는 일이 아닙니다.

여러분도 아시다시피, 북한은 여러 번 미국 시민들을 구금한 적이 있습니다. 미국은 보통 고위급 인물들을 보내야 했죠. 예를 들면, 빌 리처드슨, 또는 전직 대통령인 카터와 클린턴이 북한에 구류된 미국인들을 미국으로 송환한 적이 있습니다. 오바마 대통령 하의 북한 인권 문제 미국 특사 로버트 킹, 미국 국무부 대북정책 특별대표 특사 조셉 윤과 같은 사람들이 북한에 구금된 미국인들을 송환한 경험이 있습니다. 그런데 이는 미국 정부가 좋아하는 일은 아닙니다. 왜냐하면 이런 일이 발생하면 보통 북한에서 스파이 활동을 했다는 이유로 '사과'를 해야 하고, 그 대가로 송환된 이들에게 유감을 표명해야 하기 때문입니다. 하지만 이번 트래비스 킹 사건에서는 미국 정부가 어느정도 희망을 가지고 있었던 상황이었습니다. 미국 정부 관계자들은 킹 병사의 구금이 북한과 접촉할 기회를 제공할 수 있으며, 이 문제를 시작으로 다른 문제에 대해 논의할 수 있는 계기가 될 수 있다고 생각했습니다.

그러나 북한은 킹 병사를 송환할 준비가 되었을 때, 두 가지 조건을 제시했습니다. 첫 번째 조건은 그를 미국이 아닌 제3국으로 송환하겠다는 것이었고, 두 번째 조건은 미국과의 협상을 하지 않겠다는 것이었습니다. 결국 이 병사는 스웨덴과의 협상 끝에 송환되었습니다. 미국은 북한에 대사관을 두고 있지 않고, 스웨덴이 미국을 보호하는 대표국이기 때문입니다. 중국과의 협상도 이루어졌습니다. 이는 북한이 미국과 대화할 의향이 거의 없음을 보여주는 또 하나의 사례입니다.

결론적으로, 북한의 도발이 더 많아질 것으로 예상되며, 이런 도발에서 벗어나는 전통적인 해결책인 미국과 북한 간의 외교적 대화나 협상이 현재로서는 가능성이 낮아 보입니다. 그래서 일부 분석가들이 말한대로, 북한이 한반도에서 전쟁을 일으킬 전략적 결정을 내린 것인지에 대한 질문이 제기됩니다. 이 주장은 북한을 오랫동안 지켜본 두 명의 전문가가 제기한 것으로, 워싱턴에서 큰 파장을 일으켰고 아마 서울에서도 비슷한 파장을 일으켰을 것입니다.

제 개인적인 의견은 북한이 전쟁을 하기로 전략적 결정을 내리지는 않을 것이라고 생각합니다. 그 이유로는 네 가지가 있습니다. 첫 번째 이유는 북한이 아직 자국의 역량에 대해 충분히 자신감을 가지지 못하고 있기 때문입니다. 즉, 북한이 한국에 어떤 행동을 취했을 때, 미국의 보복에 대응할 정도의 능력이 충분하지 않습니다. 물론, 그들은 지난 몇 년 동안 훨씬 강해졌지만, 김정은은 북한이 군사적 행동을 자행해서 한국과 미국의 사상자가 나온다고 했을때, 돌아오는 미국의 보복을 막을 수 있을 정도로 충분한 자신감을 가지고 있지 않습니다. 두 번째는 한미일, 그리고 한미 군사훈련이 김정은의 군사 공격에 대해 잘못 계산하는 일이 없도록 보장하고 있다는 점입니다.

세 번째로, 만약 북한이 정말로 전쟁을 할 준비가 되어 있다면, 이를 위한 군대 동원을 나타내는 여러 가지 움직임을 감지할 수 있을 것입니다. 이러한 움직임은 정부 및 상업용 위성 이미지로 관찰될 수 있는 전쟁 준비 신호들이 될 것입니다. 북한이 진짜 전쟁 준비를 하고 있었다면, 우크라이나 전쟁을 위해 러시아에 300만 발 이상의 탄약을 팔지 않았을 것입니다. 이에 대해서는 잠시 후에 더 이야기하겠습니다. 네 번째로, 북한이 정말로 전쟁을 준비하고 있다면, 전략적 기만을 위해 한국과 평화적인 대화를 시도했을 것입니다. 즉, 전쟁을 준비하면서 한국을 전략적 기만 전술의 일환으로 끌어들였을 겁니다. 그러나 지금 북한은 그렇지 않습니다. 오히려 한국과의 관계를 분리하려 하고 있습니다. 따라서, 2024년은 분명히 매우 힘든 해가 되겠지만 그렇다고 해서 북한이 한반도에서 전쟁을 일으킬 준비를 하고 있지는 않다고 생각합니다.

이제 다음주제로 넘어가겠습니다. 러시아와 북한의 관계에 대한 이야기입니다. 상황은 매우 좋지 않지만, 북한과 러시아 사이의 새로운 관계로 인해 더 악화되었습니다. 이는 여러 관점에서 좋지 않은 소식입니다. 첫 번째로, 오늘날 북-러 관계는 북한에게 매우 유리하게 전개되고 있다는 점에서 전례가 없는 사안입니다. 제가 말씀드리고자 하는 것은 역사적으로 북한과 소련, 북한과 러시아 간의 관계는 매우 일방적이었다는 점입니다. 북한은 항상 소련이나 러시아에게 여러 가지를 부탁하는 입장이었습니다. 안전 보장, 핵 우산 제공, 대폭 지원된 연료 공급 등을 요구했죠. 소련은 북한에 시장 가격의 1/4 수준으로 연료를 제공하기도 했습니다. 또한 북한은 고르바초프, 옐친 등 여러 소련 지도자들에게 부채 탕감을 요청하기도 했습니다.

그런데, 지금은 완전히 뒤집힌 상황입니다. 이제는 푸틴이 북한의 도움이 필요합니다. 푸틴이 북한의 탄약이 필요하고, NATO 사무총장이 지난달에 말했듯이, 우크라이나 전쟁은 이제 탄약 전쟁이 되었습니다. 러시아는 매달 약 25만에서 30만 발의 포탄을 발사하고 있으며, 우크라이나는 러시아의 공격에 맞서 최소한의 방어를 하며 약 7만 5천 발의 포탄을 반격으로 발사하고 있습니다. 이는 엄청난 양입니다. 러시아는 탄약이 부족해지기 시작했지만 북한의 도움을 받으면서 상황이 바뀌었습니다. 이로 인해 북한과 러시아의 관계가 완전히 달라졌습니다. 과거에는 북한이 러시아와의 관계에서 항상 구걸하는 입장이었지만, 이제는 푸틴이 우크라이나 전쟁에서 생존하기 위해 북한의 탄약을 필요로 하는 새로운 관계가 형성되었습니다.

이러한 변화에서 두 번째로 우려되는 점은 북한이 이렇게 군수 물자를 지원을 해준 것에 대해 "러시아는 과연 무엇을 제공하고 있을까"라는 점입니다. 우리는 북한과 러시아를 연결하는 두 개의 철도 노선, 특히 두만강-가산 철도 노선의 상업적 위성 이미지를 통해 관찰할 수 있었는데, 이 노선의 활동이 급격히 증가했다는 것을 확인할 수 있었습니다. 사실, 이 노선은 북한이 3년 동안의 코로나 봉쇄 기간 동안 거의 완전히 닫혀 있었던 상태였습니다. 하지만 김정은이 지난해 봄 러시아를 방문한 이후, 두만강-가산 철도 노선의 양측 세관 지역에서 철도 차량이 급격하게 증가한 것이 목격되었습니다. 그래프로 나타내면, 일정 기간 동안 교통량이 평탄하게 유지되다가 2023년 봄에 급격히 증가하는 모습이 나타납니다. 그리고 이는 매우 높은 수준을 유지하고 있습니다. 우려되는 점은, 러시아가 북한에 식량과 연료를 제공하고 있을 가능성입니다. 북한이 지난 3년 간의 코로나 봉쇄 기간 이후 식량과 연료에 원조가 필요했기 때문입니다.

그러나 실제로 중요한 질문은 러시아가 실질적 대가로 무엇을 제공하고 있는가 입니다. 제 개인적인 생각으로는, 김정은 위원장이 2023년 봄에 러시아로 향하는 긴 여정을 하면서 단지 식량과 연료만을 위해 갔을 가능성은 낮다고 봅니다. 그래서 많은 우려가 제기되고 있는 것은 러시아가 북한에 기술, 군사 위성 기술, 핵 잠수함 기술, 탄도 미사일 기술 등을 제공하고 있을 가능성입니다. 이 부분이 매우 우려스러운 사안입니다.

이와 관련해 세 번째로 걱정스러운 소식은, 푸틴이 북한과의 새로운 관계에서 미국을 어렵게 만들 기회를 찾았다고 생각한다는 점입니다. 분명히 푸틴은 바이든 행정부가 우크라이나를 지원하는 것에 대해 불만이 많습니다. 그리고 그는 북한을 통해 미국에 세 가지 측면에서 어려움을 주는 방법을 찾았을 가능성이 큽니다. 첫 번째는 물론 우크라이나 전쟁에 필요한 탄약이지만, 또 다른 측면은 북한에 군사 기술을 제공함으로써 푸틴이 지금 북한의 대량살상무기(WMD) 능력을 향상시키는 데 도움을 주고 있다는 사실을 알고 있다는 점입니다. 이를 통해 푸틴은 미국의 안보 계산을 단지 유럽뿐만 아니라 국제적으로도 복잡하게 만드는 데 일조하고 있다는 점에서 어느 정도 만족감을 느낄 수도 있습니다.

마지막으로, 러시아와 김정은이 군사 장비 및 탄약 공동 생산

협정의 기회를 보고 있을 가능성도 있습니다. 이러한 협정을 통해 북한은 낡은 탄약 재고를 보충하고, 동시에 러시아를 위한 탄약도 생산할 수 있습니다. 이는 김정은에게 가장 좋은 상황일 수 있습니다. 그가 마지막으로 미국과 외교적 시도를 했을 때 트럼프 대통령과의 하노이 회담에서 실패를 겪었기 때문입니다. 이는 그에게 큰 외교적 실수였고, 결국 완전한 실패로 끝났습니다. 베트남에서 평양까지의 긴 여정 후, 북한은 바로 2019 팬데믹으로 접어들었고, 그 후 3년 반 동안 국경을 봉쇄했습니다. 따라서, 팬데믹이 끝난 후 김정은은 사실 체면을 세울 무언가가 필요했습니다. 싱가포르나 인도네시아, 몽골을 다시 방문하는 정도로는 부족했죠. 우리는 올해 봄이나 여름에 푸틴이 북한을 방문할 것이라고 확신합니다. 북한에게 매우 중요한 큰 진전이 될 것입니다.

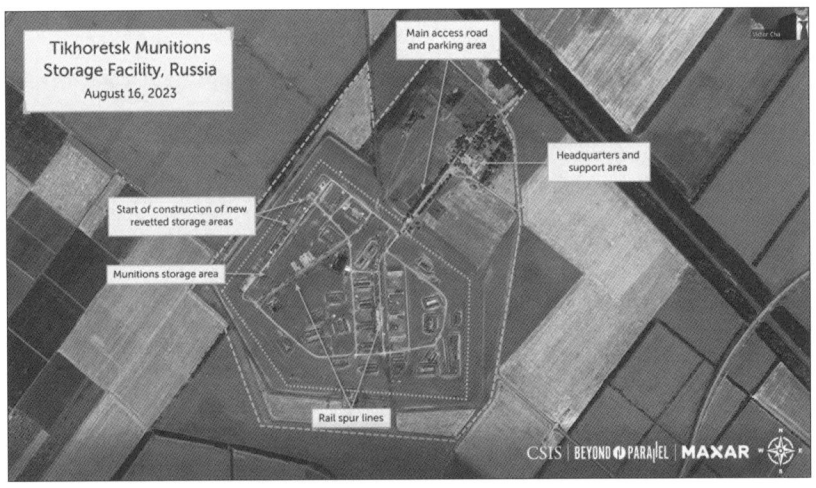

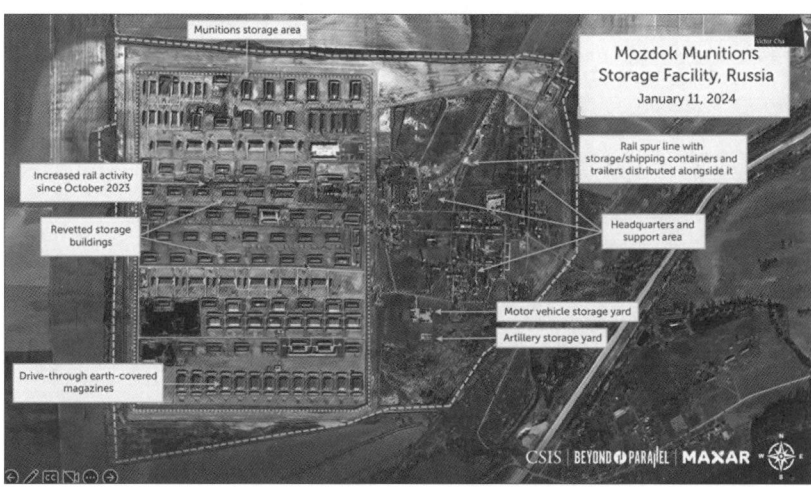

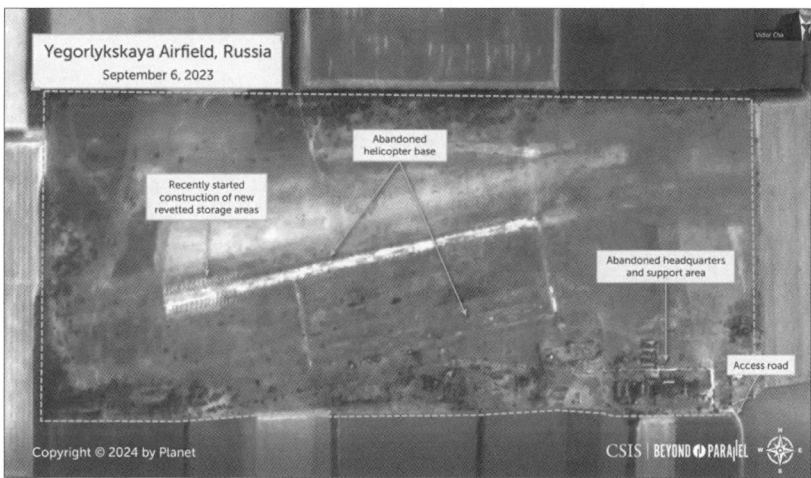

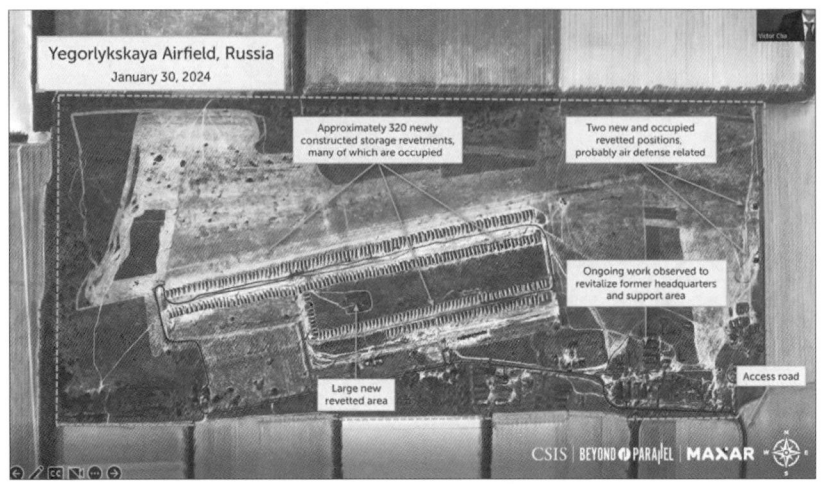

　북한이 러시아에 어떻게 물자를 공급하고 있는지 살펴보는 상업 위성 이미지를 빠르게 보여드리겠습니다. 그들이 하고 있는 일은 나진 항구에서 러시아 동쪽의 항구로 물자를 옮기고, 그 이후 러시아는 이를 육로 철도를 통해 유라시아 대륙을 가로질러 우크라이나 전선 근처의 세 개의 저장 창고로 이동시키고 있습니다. 이곳은 그 중 하나인 티코레츠크로 2023년 8월에 찍은 사진입니다. 이 사진은 2024년 2월에 찍은 같은 저장고의 사진입니다. 2023년 8월과 2024년 2월의 차이를 보면, 러시아가 정말 새로 건설한 탄약 저장고가 많이 보입니다. 이 지역은 북한의 무기로 채워진 새로운 저장고들이 들어섰습니다. 다른 예는 모즈도크입니다. 여기에서도 새해부터 북한 무기로 인한 많은 활동이 보이고 있습니다. 그리고 이곳은 러시아의 한 공항입니다. 여긴 제가 발음이 어떻게 되는지 정확히는 모르겠는데요. 사진은 2023년 9월에 찍은 것으로, 우크라이나 전선 근처에 있는 거의 버려진 공항입니다. 2023년 9월의 모습은 이렇고, 2024년 1월의 모습은 이렇습니다. 약 320개의 새로 건설된 저장 시설이 구축 되어있으며, 이 모든 것들이 북한과 러시아 간의 협력 수준을 보여주는 물리적인 증거들입니다. 백악관은 10,000개의 선적 컨테이너에 담긴 탄약을 언급했고, 한국 국방부는 3백만 발 이상의 탄약과 북한의 탄도 미사일이 우크라이나에 착륙한 사실을 밝혔습니다. 이로써 매우 깊고, 강력한 관계가 형성되고 있음을 알 수 있습니다.

가장 최근의 협력은 지난주 주말에 있었습니다. 북한이 유엔 안보리 결의안에 대해 거부권을 행사하여 유엔 전문가 패널의 임기 갱신을 막았기 때문입니다. 유엔 전문가 패널은 북한에 대한 유엔 제재 이행을 감시하는 역할을 합니다. 저는 이것이 러시아가 북한에 대한 유엔 제재 체제를 완전히 해체하려는 노력의 일환이라고 생각합니다. 이를 위한 첫 번째 단계는 더 이상 제재를 준수하지 않는 것이었습니다. 러시아는 이제까지 그들이 서명한 유엔 제재를 모두 따르지 않고 있습니다. 그 다음 단계는 전문가 패널의 임기 갱신을 차단하는 것입니다. 그리고 세 번째 단계는 그들이 북한에 대한 유엔 제재를 규정한 10개의 유엔 안보리 결의안에 대해 일몰 조항(sunset clauses)을 요구하고 있다는 것입니다.

이 모든 것이 한국과 미국에 어떤 의미가 있을까요? 여러 가지가 있겠지만, 저는 특히 한 가지에 대해 말씀드리고자 합니다. 바로 우크라이나에서 벌어진 일들이 분명히 보여준 것은, 유엔 안보리가 더 이상 규칙 기반의 국제 질서를 위한 글로벌 기구로 기능할 수 없다는 점입니다. 중국과 러시아가 유엔 안보리에서의 어떤 조치도 차단할 것이기 때문입니다.

G20은 매우 큰 그룹이고, BRICS 역시 거대 그룹이며, 두 그룹 모두 중국을 포함하고 있습니다. 그래서 점점 더 보기에, 글로벌 거버넌스를 위한 유일한 실질적인 기관은 G7, 즉 7개 주요 민주주의 국가들이 모인 그룹으로 보입니다. 이들은 유엔이 글로벌 거버넌스 기관으로서 기능하지 못하는 상황에서 정책을 조율할 수 있는 동맹국들입니다. 그러나 미국과 한국에게 중요한 G7은 현재 그 역할을 수행하기에는 부족합니다. 즉, G7은 글로벌 거버넌스를 이끌어갈 준비가 되어 있지 않으며, 이를 위해서는 G7의 확장이 필요합니다. 제가 말씀드리는 G7의 확장은 한국, 호주, 심지어 스페인과 같은 다른 유럽 국가들이 포함되어야 한다는 의미입니다. 이 국가들이 포함 되어야만 G7이 현재의 글로벌 거버넌스의 위기를 해결하는 중요한 역할을 할 수 있습니다. 우크라이나 전쟁과 북한에 대한 제재가 보여주듯이, 이제 유엔은 그 역할을 수행할 수 없게 되었습니다.

제 강연은 여기까지입니다. 이제 관련 질문들을 받겠습니다. 감사합니다.

전광우 이사장: 네, 박사님. 훌륭한 강연에 감사드립니다. 매우 포괄적인 발표였습니다. 또한 한반도에서 우리가 직면한 중요한 문제들을 잘 다뤄 주셨습니다. 북한의 도발이 증가하고 있으며, 전 세계적으로 선거가 많은 2024년에는 더 심화될 것이라는 점을 명확히 언급해 주셨습니다. 이러한 상황 속에서 한미일 3국 동맹 강화되고 있는 점은 긍정적이나 다른 한편으로 북한과 러시아 간의 동맹이 강화에서 기인되는 매우 우려스러운 상황도 지적해주셨습니다. 복잡하고 어려운 부분에 대해 명확하게 설명해 주셔서 감사

드립니다.

이제 질의응답 시간을 갖겠습니다. 오늘은 두 분의 토론자를 모셨습니다. 먼저 허경욱 대사님을 소개해 드리겠습니다. 대사님께서는 기재부 제1차관을 비롯해 정부 고위직을 두루 역임하셨으며, 한국의 OECD 대사를 지내셨습니다. 세계은행과 IMF에도 재직하셨습니다.

허경욱 대사: 차 박사님, 훌륭한 발표 감사합니다. 매우 정확한 상황을 보여주셨지만, 동시에 북한의 위협이 증가하고 있다는 상당히 암울한 전망을 보여주셨습니다. 북한에 대해 논의할 때 문제는 항상 부정적인 상황, 혹은 더 부정적인 상황, 혹은 최악의 선택지만 남는다는 점입니다. 그러면서, 일부 미국 정계에서는 김정은이 전쟁을 치를 수도 있다는 입장이 있다고 말씀을 하셨습니다만, 이것이 아직 뒷받침할 만한 증거가 없다라는 말씀도 하셨습니다.

그런데 동시에, 우리에게는 두 가지 큰 우려 사항이 있습니다. 첫 번째는 국내 이슈입니다. 북한의 도발이 심화되고 있고 북-러의 위험한 동맹이 강화되는 상황에도 불구하고, 한국 사회의 일부에서는 '평화가 무엇보다 중요하다'는 순진한 시각이 존재합니다. 이들은 아마도 북한의 위협이 캠프 데이비드 선언에서 비롯된 것일 수 있다고 생각하는데, 저는 전혀 동의하지 않지만, 그런 생각을 가진 이들이 한국 사회의 일부에 늘어나고 있는 것은 우려스러운 일입니다. 이 부분에 대한 의견을 듣고 싶습니다.

그리고 두 번째로, G7 확대가 필요하다는 말씀을 하셨는데, 다가오는 미국 대선에서 트럼프가 다시 대통령으로 당선된다면, 그가 결국 거래를 선호한다는 점에 대한 우려가 커지고 있습니다. 그리고 만약 트럼프가 북한과 우리를 배제한 채 거래를 한다면, 특히 미국이 주한미군을 철수하거나 축소할 결정을 내린다면, 우리는 어떤 선택을 해야 할까요? 그런 상황이 온다면 이제 한국도 진지하게 핵무기 개발을 고려해야 한다는 목소리가 커지고 있습니다. 만약 그런 상황이 발생할 가능성이 있다면, 그 가능성이 얼마나 될지, 그리고 국제 사회가 한국의 핵무기 개발을 받아들일 수 있을지에 대해 두 가지 질문을 드리겠습니다. 감사합니다.

빅터 차 박사: 허 대사님, 좋은 질문 감사합니다. 시간이 많지 않은 관계로 간단하게 답변을 드리겠습니다. 먼저 캠프 데이비드 관련 질문에 대해 말씀드리겠습니다. "캠프 데이비드가 결국 북한 도발 행위의 원인이 되고 있는가"라는 질문이었는데요. 사실 제가 발표를 시작하면서 보여드린 데이터를 보시면 북한의 도발 행위는 캠프 데이비드 정상회담 전부터 시작되었다는 것을 보실 수 있습니다. 또, 도발을 단행하는 명확한 원인은 발표에서 말씀드린 대로, 과학적인 이유와 실전 훈련에 있다는 것입니다. 따라서 캠프 데이비드와는 상관이 없다고 생각합니다. 저도 이 두 가지가 연결되어 있다고 주장하는 사람들이 있다는 점은 알고 있습니다만, 북한이 지금 이렇게 강도 높은 도발을 계속하는 데에는 전혀 다른 독립적인 이유들이 있다는 점을 말씀드리고 싶습니다.

트럼프와 관련된 질문에 대해서는, 2025년에 누가 백악관을 차지하게 되든, 북한의 입장은 크게 달라지지 않을 것이라고 생각합니다. 즉, 우크라이나 전쟁과 가자 지구 상황에도 불구하고, 이 문제는 새로 당선되는 대통령에게 가장 중요한 이슈가 될 것입니다. 그러나 트럼프의 첫 번째 임기 동안 그와 이야기했던 사람들과의 대화를 통해 제가 느낀 점은, 트럼프가 2017년의 '화염과 분노(fire and fury)' 전략으로 돌아갈 가능성은 낮다는 것입니다. 김정은과의 외교를 계속 이어나갈 가능성이 더 크다고 생각합니다.

그리고 제재 완화를 대가로 장거리 탄도 미사일 시험과 핵 실험을 하지 않겠다고 하는 거래를 시도할 가능성도 있지만, 비핵화나 단거리 탄도 미사일, 또는 한국에 위협이 될 만한 다른 것들은 포함되지 않을 것입니다. 이것이 바로 '디커플링'이죠. 이런 형태의 디커플링은 한국에서 심각한 우려를 불러일으킬 것이며, 한국이 앞으로 무엇을 해야 할지에 대한 국가 안보 논의를 촉발할 수 있을 것입니다.

전광우 이사장: 네 감사합니다. 그럼 다음 토론자 고려대학교 김진일 교수님을 모시겠습니다. 김 교수님께서는 예일대에서 석박사 학위를 취득하셨고 미국 연준에서 활약하셨고, 조지타운 대학교 등에서도 많은 경험과 경력을 쌓아오신 명성이 높으신 경제학자이십니다. 자, 그럼 김 교수님을 환영해 주시기 바랍니다.

김진일 교수: 감사합니다 이사장님. 차 박사님 안녕하세요. 훌륭한 강연 감사드립니다. 저는 앞서 허 대사님이 언급하신 마지막 질문, 즉 선거와 관련된 질문을 이어가겠습니다. 트럼프 시

나리오에 대해서는 저는 무역 문제에 대해 여쭤보고 싶습니다. 외교 측면에서는 트럼프가 과거에 했던 일을 이어갈 것이라고 말씀하셨는데, 무역은 그보다 조금 더 복잡한 문제라고 생각합니다. 우리가 생각해봐야 할 주요한 무역 이슈는 무엇일까요? 만약 트럼프가 당선된다면, 특히 중국과의 무역 문제에서 어떤 일이 일어날까요? 한국이 아마도 중국과 미국의 영향을 가장 많이 받는 나라일 텐데, 이에 대한 교수님의 의견을 들어보고 싶습니다.

빅터 차 박사: 네, 질문 감사드립니다. 먼저 동맹국에 대한 트럼프의 생각은 아마 변하지 않을 것이라 생각합니다. 그는 여전히 동맹국들을 무역 경쟁자로 보고 있습니다. 그리고 미국과 무역 흑자를 보고 있는 어떤 나라나 동맹국에 대해서는, 한국도 포함이겠지만, 아마 트럼프는 관세를 부과할 것입니다. 터무니없게 들릴 수도 있지만 10%의 세금을 일괄적으로 부과할 가능성이 높습니다. 중국과 관련해서는 아마 두 가지 정도의 시나리오가 나올 것 같습니다.

사실, 공화당 예비선거에서 온건파 공화당원들, 예를 들어 니키 헤일리 같은 인물들이 이런 견해를 표명한 적이 있습니다. 일부 공화당 내에서는 중국에 대한 PNTR(항구적 정상 무역 관계) 철회를 주장하는 목소리가 나오고 있습니다. 즉, 중국과의 무역을 정말로 강경하게 분리하려는 입장이죠. 이런 점에서 트럼프는 그보다 더 온건한 입장을 취할 수도 있습니다. 그는 첫 번째 임기 때처럼 높은 세금을 부과할 수는 있지만, PNTR을 철회하자고 주장하는 수준까지는 가지 않을 가능성이 큽니다.

경제 안보 문제에 있어서는 바이든 행정부와의 연속성이 있을 것이라고 생각합니다. 반도체, AI, 양자 컴퓨팅에 대해서는, 저는 바이든 행정부가 했던 정책을 계속 이어갈 것이라고 확신합니다. 트럼프는 그 정책을 시작한 사람이 결국은 자신이라고 생각할 것이기 때문에, 바이든 행정부에서 했던 일을 크게 바꾸지 않고 계속 이어갈 가능성이 큽니다. 실제로 트럼프 행정부에서도 BRI 금융이나 화웨이 5G 문제에서 중국과의 디커플링을 시도하는 노력이 있었죠. 이 점을 미루어 보면 따라서 중국의 입장에서는 트럼프가 재집권해도 트럼프의 첫 임기와 유사한 행보를 아마 기대를 해야 될 것 같습니다.

중국은 바이든 행정부가 지금까지 공급망 안전성 확보와 관련해서 이룬 성과에 대해 매우 우려하고 있습니다. 그리고 트럼프가 재집권하게 된다면 상황이 더욱 복잡해질 것입니다. 개인적으로는 아마 시진핑 주석과 계속 대화를 하고 전략적인 개입과 관계에 대해서 이야기를 할 것이라고 생각합니다. 그러나 경제적인 측면에서는, 경쟁구도가 계속 이어질 것으로 보입니다. 감사합니다.

전광우 이사장: 좋은 답변 감사드립니다. 이제 마지막으로 저희 시청자분들을 위해 박사님께 몇 가지 질문을 더 드리겠습니다.

첫 번째는 대만 상황과 관련된 질문입니다. 실제로 지난주, 제가 이해한 바로는, 미국 의회에서 중요한 발언과 증언이 나왔습니다. 인도-태평양 사령관인 존 아퀼리노 제독은 중국이 2027

년까지 대만 침공 준비를 진행하고 있는 것으로 보인다고 말했습니다. 이는 시진핑 주석의 세 번째 임기가 끝나기 바로 1년 전입니다. 그럼, 이 상황이 얼마나 심각하고, 향후 몇 년 안에 어떻게 전개될지에 대한 교수님의 의견을 듣고 싶습니다. 이는 한반도의 평화에 매우 심각한 영향을 미칠 수밖에 없으리라 생각합니다.

두 번째 질문은 미 대선 결과에 따른 한미일 3국 관계의 향방입니다. 일부에서는 트럼프가 승리한다면 한미일 3국 연합 관계가 바이든 하에서와 같이 유지되지 않을 것이라고 예상하고 있습니다. 교수님께서는 어떻게 전개될 것으로 보시는지 궁금합니다.

마지막으로, 트럼프가 재집권 하게 될 경우, 동북아 안보 체계에 어떤 긍정적인 측면이 있을 수 있을까요? 많은 사람들이 트럼프의 승리에 따른 위험 요소와 그 영향에 대해 이야기하지만, 저는 그 반대의 가능성도 고려할 필요가 있다고 생각합니다.

빅터 차 박사: 이사장님, 좋은 질문 감사합니다. 마지막 질문과 초반에 말씀하신 내용을 연결해서 답변 드리겠습니다. 우선 G7 확대, 즉 한국, 호주와 같은 국가들을 포함시키는 것이 트럼프에게 G7에 대한 특별한 도장을 찍는 기회가 될 수 있다고 설득할 수 있을 것입니다. 기억하시겠지만, 트럼프는 G7과, 특히 독일 메르켈 총리와 매우 적대적인 관계를 유지했었죠. 그리고 유럽에 대해서는 방위비 지출을 늘려야 한다고 불만을 털어놓기도 했습니다. 하지만 그가 한국, 호주, 스페인과 같은 국가들을 포함하여 G7을 G10으로 확장하는 것을 G7에 대해서 특별 인장을 찍는 것과 같은 행위일 것입니다. 결국 그가 '자신이 한 일'이라고

할 수 있는 어떤 일이든, 그는 그것을 좋아할 가능성이 큽니다. 그래서 이것이 하나의 기회라고 생각합니다.

또 다른 기회는, 트럼프가 동맹국 방위에 많은 비용을 지출하는 것을 원하지 않을 것이라는 점입니다. 그는 많은 군사 훈련을 중단하려 할 것이고, 이런 점에서 한국에게 기회가 될 수도 있습니다. 저는 한국이 자국 방위비나 군사 장비 구매와 관련해서 거의 아무런 제약도 받지 않을 것이라고 생각합니다. 대만 문제와 관련해서도 마찬가지입니다.

대만 문제에 대해선, 예, 매우 우려되는 상황입니다. 미국 인도-태평양 사령관이 중국이 2027년까지 대만 침공을 준비하고 있다고 한 것에 대해, 우리는 이 문제를 매우 진지하게 받아들여야 합니다. 제가 두 가지를 언급하고 싶은데, 첫 번째는 시진핑이 현재 대만 해협에서 전쟁을 실제로 벌일 수 있을 만큼 자국 군에 대한 자신감을 가지고 있지 않다는 점입니다. 현재 그는 군 내 부패 문제에 매우 신경 쓰고 있으며, 군의 전투력에 대한 신뢰를 전혀 갖고 있지 않습니다. 이런 면에서 저는 시진핑이 준비되어 있지 않다고 생각합니다.

또한 그는 우크라이나 전쟁에서 참혹한 피해 상황을 보고 있습니다. 중국, 중국 국민, 중국 정부, 중국 군대는 한국 전쟁 이후로 전쟁에서 인명 피해를 본 적이 없다는 것을 기억해야 합니다. 그런데 대만에서 이렇게 전쟁을 하게 될 경우에는 사상자가 대량으로 발생하게 될 것이고. 중국에게 있어서는 큰 손해를 가져올 것입니다. 그리고 보다 우려해야 될 부분은 잘 아시는 것처럼 대만 신정부가 5월 출범하게 된다는 점입니다. 우리는 윌리엄 라이의 정치적 성향에 대해 잘 알지 못합니다. 그는 외교 정책에 집중하지 않고 있으며, 교차 해협 관계에 대해서도 강한 입장을 보이지 않고 있습니다. 다만 우리는 그가 약간의 민족주의적 본능을 가지고 있다는 점을 잘 알고 있습니다. 만약 그가 갑자기 매우 도발적인 발언을 한다면, 시진핑은 그에 대해 조치를 취하게 될 것입니다. 그럴 경우 미국이 중요한 역할을 해야 한다고 생각합니다. 그런 시나리오가 현실이 되지 않도록 하는 역할말입니다.

전광우 이사장: 네, 감사합니다. 오늘 훌륭한 강연을 해주시고 토론시간에도 최선을 다해 해주셔서 진심으로 감사드립니다. 다음에는 꼭 직접 뵐 기회가 마련되기를 바랍니다.

빅터 차 박사: 감사합니다.

Geopolitical Challenges for East Asia with the 2024 US Presidential Election: Implications for S. Korea's Diplomatic and Security Policies

Victor Cha

Victor Cha

Dr. Cha is currently a professor and Vice Dean at Georgetown University. He is also Senior Vice President and Korea Chair at CSIS, the Center for Strategic and International Studies. Dr. Cha is former Director for Asian Affairs at the White House National Security Council, and has served as President George W. Bush's top advisor on North Korean affairs.

[Apr. 2, 2024]

Geopolitical Challenges for East Asia with the 2024 US Presidential Election: Implications for S. Korea's Diplomatic and Security Policies

Victor Cha
Distinguished University Professor, Georgetown University
Senior Vice President for Asia and Korea Chair, CSIS

Jun Kwang-woo: Good morning, ladies and gentlemen. Welcome to the IGE Forum.

Today, we are most fortunate to have an outstanding guest speaker, Dr. Victor Cha, a leading authority on US foreign policy, especially regarding Asia. He will be joining us live from Washington D.C. to discuss key diplomatic and security issues in the face of rising geopolitical challenges, including US-China tensions, North Korea's provocations, and the deepening alliance between North Korea and Russia. We expect he will also explore strategic implications for South Korea. Dr. Cha's opening speech will reflect on the recent significant developments with regard to security on the Korean peninsula.

Dr. Cha is currently a Distinguished University Professor

at Georgetown University, and also Senior Vice President for Asia and Korea Chair at CSIS (the Center for Strategic and International Studies). Dr. Cha is former Director for Asian Affairs for the White House's National Security Council, and has served as President George W. Bush's top advisor on North Korean affairs. He holds a PhD in Political Science from Columbia University and in 2023, was named the Distinguished University Professor, the highest honor bestowed upon a tenured faculty at Georgetown University.

Without further ado, let's welcome Dr. Victor Cha who will speak first for about 30 minutes, followed by the discussion and Q&A as scheduled.

Victor Cha: Thank you very much, Dr. Jun. I'm very happy to be part of the IGE webinar again. As Dr. Jun said, I'd like to start out my remarks closer to home for all of you on the Korean Peninsula talking about what the security situation looks like there. Then branch out from there and talk a little bit about the relationship with Russia, and then close by saying what it may mean for South Korea. I'm happy to, in the discussion, speculate about our politics and United States, what will happen in our election and what that could mean for the alliance relationship. But I'll leave that for the Q&A rather than giving a presentation on that particular aspect of it.

So where I'd like to begin is to talk a little bit about what we should expect to see from North Korea in 2024, what the likelihood there is of conflict, of some have even speculated war coming from North Korea in 2024. And I've brought along some data with me this morning, this evening, to try to address this question of what to expect from North Korea in 2024. The bottom line up front is that I certainly expect, and we've already seen, much more belligerent North Korea in 2024. In fact, I think just today or over your evening last night, North Korea fired another ballistic missile into the into the direction of Japan. I expect we'll see a lot more of this in 2024 with really little opportunity for dialogue. I don't think dialogue is impossible, but as things stand right now, they don't look very plausible given the current situation. And let me explain why I feel that way. And I'm going to share my screen here so that you can see some of my slides. I think you can see that.

So the situation right now is what we've seen has been a secular increase in North Korean provocations over the years, over the past four US administrations. So what you see here on your screen is the average annual number of provocations by North Korea during each year of the past four presidencies in the United States. So if we start at the far left, we see that during George W. Bush, the average was about three and a half North Korean major military provocations per year. As Dr. Jun mentioned, this was the administration that I served in in the united states. And I was surprised by this number because it certainly felt like more than three and a half a year. It felt more like three and a half every month or every other month. But nevertheless, if we look at it over eight years of the George W. Bush administration there are about three and a half major military provocations by North Korea per year.

If we move then to the Obama, the eight years of the Obama administration, we see this go up to just about almost 11 provocations per year as you're probably aware the Obama administration was known for a policy of what was called strategic patience which wasn't focused so much on diplomacy, but was focused on sanctions pressure on North Korea to try to put them in a position where they would be more pliable for negotiations. And so during this period, we saw almost about 11 provocations per year.

If we move next to the Donald Trump administration, the four years of Donald Trump, the number is just about 10 provocations per year. This to me was also surprising because of course the Trump years were known for the summit diplomacy with Kim Jong-un, but in spite of that summit diplomacy, the actual average number of provocations was not that different from the eight years of Obama when there was no summit diplomacy. They were about the same, which I think itself is interesting. And then of course the really interesting thing is when we get to the Biden administration, we see this dramatic increase to an average annual of 34 major military demonstrations, ballistic missile tests, cruise missile tests, things of this nature. 34, average annual of 34 per year, which is a dramatic, dramatic increase.

If you see in this next slide, we've broken this down for you by year between the four years of Biden, which we are now completing, and the four years of Trump. You can see, if we go to the very bottom of the slide in 2017, the Trump administration, you'll remember 2017 was the year of fire and fury. where there was a lot of talk, loose talk between Trump and Kim threatening each other, Trump calling Kim a little rocket man, promising to rain "fire and fury" on North Korea. Kim jong-un responding that Trump was senile and that North Korea was ready to strike targets of major U.S. Cities. 2017, as you remember, was a very difficult year with lots of the potential for things escalating out of control.

Then we see in 2018, we see that this is the when the summit meeting started this Singapore summit in 2018 and then the beginning of 2019 the Hanoi summit and we see actually no provocations in 2018. In fact, in all of the data that we've collected on North Korean belligerent behavior this is the only year in which there are no provocations There are no belligerent acts by North Korea, 2018, during the year of summit diplomacy with Trump. But as we all know, in 2019, that summit diplomacy fails after the Hanoi summit in February 2019, where Donald Trump leaves the summit meeting without an agreement. He actually cuts the summit meeting short without an agreement. And North Korea goes back to its practices of continuing these provocations through 2020.

If we go now to the Biden administration, we see in 2021, initially North Korea did some provocations, but there weren't that many. And I think that was in large part because they were in a wait and see mode, trying to see what the policy review of the Biden administration would turn up with regard to policy towards North Korea. And they basically gave the Biden administration one year from inauguration in January of 2021 to January of 2022. They gave them basically one year to try to understand what the policy would be. And then almost like clockwork in January of 2022, it's almost like someone turned a switch in North Korea, and then they went back into full scale and a dramatically heightened tempo of military provocations, missile provocations, and other sorts of military provocations. 51 in the year of 2022, '29 and the year of 2023. And they're already on pace in 2024 to do quite a large number of these sorts of actions.

So this is what I mean when I say that there's been this dramatic increase, steady increase over time in North Korean behavior. And the question, of course, is why? why we're seeing this. And I think there are three reasons.

The first has to do with the science of missile demonstrations and testing. North Korea right now, Kim Jong-un is right now in the process of perfecting, developing and perfecting different varieties of missiles cruise missiles, ballistic technology, mobile launched missiles, solid propellant missiles, countermeasures on ballistic missiles, hypersonic warheads, multiple reentry vehicles on a single warhead. There are a whole suite of capabilities that he is trying to develop now. And in order to accomplish that, he needs to test. So these missile demonstrations, on the one hand, the heightened number of them has to do with science and development and a testing timetable in order to perfect these capabilities. And that's why we're seeing more of them. Kim Jong-un has made very clear a long list of things that he is trying to acquire in terms of missile and nuclear capabilities. So they need to test these things in order to collect data, to try to understand whether they're doing things correctly, if they need to make adjustments. There's only a limited amount that you can do through computer simulation. They need to actually do the testing. So that's certainly one reason, science and development.

Another reason has to do with really more operational exercising. And what I mean here is that certainly some of the heightened testing has to do with science and development, but some of it is not about science and development and it actually is focused more on operational exercising. So when North Korea is testing the same missile over and over again, whether it's a short range ballistic missile or a medium range one, one that they seemingly have already done a number of tests on, then you have to start thinking this is not just science. This is not just development and science. This is now moving into the realm of exercising. So when they fire a short range ballistic missile or a series of them, and then they follow it with medium range ballistic missile tests, and they follow it with a bomber run, then that When you put those things together, that is military exercising. That's operational exercising, just like the US and South Korea do exercising. This is North Korea exercising standoff capabilities or nuclear attack capabilities, for all we know, with their short-range and medium-range ballistic missiles. So that's another reason why I think we're seeing heightened testing under or the Biden administration.

And then the third reason I think we're seeing this high degree of testing has to do with diplomacy or I should say the lack of diplomacy between the United States and North Korea. We've done a study at CSIS that looks back, goes all the way back to the days of the agreed framework in the 1990s and found that there is definitely an observable correlation between periods of US DPRK negotiations or diplomacy and a lowered tempo of North Korean testing, missile demonstrations, other sorts of belligerent acts. In other words, in periods when the United States and North Korea are sitting at the table together, either in a multilateral six-party format or bilaterally, those periods coincide with a much lower tempo or even no North Korean provocations. And so the flip side of that is that we have not had any real negotiations for quite some time now. We've had no negotiations really in the Biden administration at all. We haven't seen any negotiations and therefore we're seeing heightened testing by North Korea. So I think those are some of the reasons why we've sort of seen this secular increase from the George W. Bush administration through Obama, through Trump, and now to the Biden administration.

So with that, this gets to my next point, which is that in 2024, I think things are things will get even worse. I expect to see a heightened tempo of testing, of demonstrations, of exercising, And the first reason has to do with 2024 itself. 2024, as you all know, I mean, it's an election year in Korea. You have an election coming up very soon in nine days. I guess it's eight days because it's April 2nd there. But of course, in the United States, we have an election in November. And one of the things that we found again in our collection of data is that there is an observable correlation between U.S. presidential election years and a heightened pattern of North Korean missile demonstrations and belligerent actions. That is, in years when the United States has a presidential election or when the United States has a congressional election without a presidential election, those are the so-called midterm elections. In those particular election years, we tend to see much more North Korean activity.

And so I can, if I share with you just one other slide. If I share with you just one other slide. So this shows the average number of provocations under Kim Jong Il and under Kim Jong Un in a U.S. election year, during major U.S. election years. So the Kim Jong-un data set goes from 1996 to 2010, and the Kim Jong-un data set goes from 2012 to 2022. And this is including both presidential and midterm election years. We see that you can see right here that there's a dramatic increase, that Kim Jong-un is much more active during major US election years than his father was. So there is a relationship there too between US elections and North Korean provocations. I think North Korea does this in order to position themselves well in advance of the, in advance of whoever becomes the president in 2025, whether it's Biden or whether it's Trump again, by ramping up the provocations, they seek to gain leverage, seek to make themselves an urgent foreign policy matter for their new administration, and to use that as leverage to try to extract concessions as soon as the new administration comes in.

Another reason I think that we're seeing this 2024, we'll see a lot more provocations has to do with, particularly in the first quarter and second quarter of this year, has to do with U.S. military exercising. The United States is now in a heightened tempo of US military exercising around the Korean Peninsula with South Korea. And then there also are new trilateral exercises that will take place between the United States, Japan, and South Korea. Again, all of the data shows that North Korea feels compelled to respond to those provocations as they have done in the past month. And so that's just a pattern we expect to continue, particularly as the United States continues to ramp up all of this exercising.

So that's what I wanted to share in terms of data. Now, in terms of policy, so this heightened exercising that we'll see in 2024, I do not think is the fault of the Biden administration. They have been trying consistently through many different channels to try to engage with North Korea over the past four years. I've been told informally that they have sought at least on 20 separate channels separate occasions to make contact, to present proposals to the North Koreans to come back to the negotiating table, whether this was on nuclear weapons, on sanctions relief, on COVID vaccines, on food, on fuel, a whole host of things. And there has been absolutely no North Korean response of any substance whatsoever. So the North Koreans clearly are not interested in talking to the United States. That seems to be pretty clear.

And one example of this, recent example of this that many of you probably read about in the newspapers was when the North Koreans made the decision to return Travis King, a U.S., US soldier who was being escorted out, a US soldier who was stationed in South Korea and was being on his way to being deported out of the country to what would probably have been a dishonorable discharge from the US military. He escaped from Incheon Airport and then went on a DMZ tour and then ran across the DMZ into North Korea in the joint security area. The North Koreans first isolated Private King for a period of time in order to ensure that there was no transmission of the COVID virus because North Korea still remains one of two countries that does not have any COVID vaccine infrastructure in the country. And then after that, they interrogated him for a couple of months and then they wanted to send him back to the United States. back to the United States. This is not the first time.

As you all know, North Korea has detained US citizens. They've done it many times in the past. And the United States has usually had to send somebody, a fairly high level public figure. It could be Bill Richardson. It could have been former presidents Carter and Clinton. Both have brought back Americans. People like Robert King, the U.S. Special Envoy for North Korean Human Rights Issues under President Obama, and Joseph Yun, the U.S. State Department's Special Representative for North Korea Policy, have repatriated Americans detained in North Korea. And this is something that the US government does not like to do because when they do, when this does happen, they usually have to issue some sort of bogus apology, have to express regret for having, in quotation marks, been caught spying on North Korea as the price for bringing these individuals back. But in this case, in the case of Travis King, there was actually some hope by U.S. officials that this detaining of King might provide an opportunity to have contact with North Korea on Travis King, but as an opportunity or a springboard for further discussions on other issues.

But what became clear when the North Koreans were ready to return this individual, they communicated that they wanted to return him on two conditions. The first condition was that he'd be sent from North Korea to a third country, in other words, not the United States. And secondly, that they did not want to negotiate with the United States. So this individual was eventually released after negotiations with Sweden, who is the US protecting power in North Korea, since the United States doesn't have an embassy in North Korea, and with China, which was, again, a sign of how little the North Koreans had an interest in talking to the United States.

So, the bottom line is that we will see more provocations and the sort of traditional exit ramp from these provocations, which is some sort of U.S.-DPRK diplomacy or talks, don't appear to be likely at this moment. So, this then raises the question of whether, as some analysts have said, North Korea has made a strategic decision to go to war on the Korean peninsula. This was an argument that two longtime observers of North Korea have made that created quite a stir in Washington, probably created a similar stir in Seoul.

My own view on this is that I do not think that North Korea has made the strategic decision to go to war. I believe they said that These authors said in the first paragraph that Kim Jong-un has made a strategic decision like his grandfather Kim Il-sung to conduct a war on the Korean peninsula. I don't think that that's right. And I don't think it's right for four reasons. The first is that I do not believe that. So the first is that I believe that North Korea is still not confident enough in its capabilities such that it believes it can deter US retaliation to any sort of North Korean action against South Korea. Yes, their capabilities have grown much stronger over the past few years, but still they are nowhere near, Kim Jong-un is nowhere near confident enough to believe that his capabilities are sufficient to actually deter the United States from retaliating if North Korea carried out a military action that killed South Koreans and Americans. Second, the heightened tempo of U.S.-South Korea exercising as well as U.S.-South Korea-Japan exercising ensures that there is no miscalculation on the part of Kim Jong-un that somehow, he would be able to deter the United States and South Korea from responding to a military attack of any sort.

Third, if North Korea really were ready to go to war, then they would be undertaking a series of things on the ground that would be observable through both government and commercial satellite imagery that would be telltale signs of a military that was mobilizing for war. Not least of which is that if North Korea were really preparing for war, it would not be selling all of its ammunition to Russia for the war in Ukraine. They would not be selling all of this ammunition, over 3 million rounds of ammunition to Putin for the war in Ukraine if Kim Jong-un were really preparing for war. And I'll talk more about that in a minute.

And then fourth, I think that if North Korea were really

ready to engage in war on the Korean peninsula, then it would be using strategic deception by talking about peace initiatives with South Korea. They would be trying to engage South Korea as a part of their strategic deception tactics in advance of a military war. But that, of course, is not what they're doing now. If anything, they are decoupling from South Korea. So for all these reasons, I think 2024 will certainly be a very bad year. There won't be many opportunities for exit ramps, but I don't think it means that North Korea is ready to go to war on the peninsula.

Now, let me move on to the other topic, which is Russia and North Korea. So this situation that I described to you is of course not a very good one at all, but it has been made worse by this new relationship between North Korea and Russia. This is bad news in several different respects. The first is that the relationship between Russia and North Korea today is really unprecedented in favor of North Korea. And what I mean by that is that historically, the relationship between North Korea and the Soviet Union, North Korea and Russia was very one-sided in the sense that the North Koreans were always asking for things from the Soviet Union, from Russia. They were asking for security guarantees. They were asking for a nuclear umbrella. They were asking for heavily subsidized fuel. The Soviet Union used to provide fuel to North Korea at heavily subsidized prices, one quarter of the market price. And they were always asking the Soviet Union for debt relief, whether this was with Gorbachev or

Yeltsin or any others. These were sort of the things that the North Koreans were always asking the Soviet Union or Russia for.

Now we're in a completely different situation where it's Putin that needs North Korean help. It's Putin that needs North Korean ammunition. As the NATO Secretary General said last month, the Ukraine war has come down to a war of ammunition. And Russia is firing some estimate between 250,000 and 300,000 rounds of artillery every month, while the Ukrainians are trying to at least hold the line against Russia by returning fire at a burn rate of about 75,000 rounds per month. That's a lot of ammunition and Russia was running out of ammunition until it got help from North Korea. And so, this has really changed the terms of the relationship. This was one in the past where North Korea was a supplicant in the relationship. And now we have a new relationship in which Putin literally needs North Korean ammunition to survive, to survive in this war against Ukraine.

The second piece of bad news related to this is what the Russians are providing in return for all of this ammunition. And so we have been looking with commercial imagery at the North Korea. the two-railway links between North Korea and Russia. And it's very clear that activity on the Dmangang-Kasan Railroad link has increased dramatically. It was basically completely dead during the three-year COVID lockdown that North Korea was under. But just as Kim Jong-un made his trip to Russia last spring, we see a dramatic uptick in rail cars on either side, on the customs area on either side of the Dmangang Railway crossing, kha san Dangang railway crossing. If you were to graph it on a map, the level of traffic is kind of sitting flat for a period of time until the spring of 2023 when it shoots up like this. It goes straight up and it stays at that very, very high level. And so the concern here is that of course, we'd expect the Russians are providing food and fuel to North Korea because North Korea needed a great deal of this after the three year COVID lockdown.

But the real question and concern is what else are the Russians providing in return for all of this ammunition? It's my personal view that I don't think Kim Jong-un, the North Korean leader, would have traveled taking the long train ride to Russia in the spring of 2023, about a year ago, only for food and fuel. I don't think the North Korean leader would travel all the way to Russia only for food and fuel. And so there's a lot of concern that Russia might be providing technology, military satellite technology, nuclear submarine technology, ballistic missile technology to North Korea, which would be very concerning.

The third piece of bad news related to this is that I think Putin really sees an opportunity in this new relationship with North Korea to make things difficult for the united states. Obviously, Ptin is not happy with the Biden administration and their support of Ukraine. And I think he believes he's found in North Korea a great way to make things difficult for the United States in three respects. The first, of course, is ammunition that he needs for the war in Ukraine. But also through the provision of military technology to North Korea, Putin probably takes some pleasure in knowing that he is now complicating the U.S. security calculus, not just in Europe, but also internationally. Asia by providing this ability for North Korea to improve their WMD capabilities. And then third, it wouldn't surprise me if Russia also see, and Kim Jong-un, also see an opportunity in terms of military equipment and ammunition co-production arrangements, where North Korea can replenish its own very old stocks of ammunition by entering into co-production arrangements with Russia, where they can produce ammunition for themselves as well as for Russia.

And then finally, this is, I think, about the best thing that could have happened for Kim Jong-un. Because if you think about it, the last time we saw him was in the failed diplomatic gambit with the United States, where Kim Jong-un met. with President Trump in Hanoi and failed miserably. It was a big diplomatic gambit, a very big gamble for the North Korean leader that ended up being a complete failure. Long train ride from Vietnam back to Pyongyang and then went straight into the pandemic in 2019, where North Korea remained shut down for three, three and a half years. So coming out of the pandemic, Kim Jong Un, frankly, needed something big. He needed something big to save face. And, you know, another visit to Singapore or to Indonesia or to Mongolia wasn't going to do it. It had to be something big. It had to be with either China or with Russia. And of course, this is happening with Russia. We fully expect that Putin will make a return visit to North Korea. Korea sometime in the spring or the summer. So these are very big and important steps for North Korea.

I wanted to show you, just to give you a sense of this cooperation, and I know I'm running short on time, I wanted to show you just quickly some of the commercial satellite image that we have been using to look at how North Korea has been supplying Russia. What they're doing is they're moving things from Najim port to Dane port in Russia on the east side of the continent. And then Russia is moving it by land, by railway west, all the way across the width of the Eurasian continent to three storage depots that are near the war front with the Ukraine, Ukraine. This is one of them, Tikoretsk. This is a picture of Tikoretsk in August of 2023. So you can see this storage facility here.

And this is a picture of the same storage facility in February of 2024. So this is February 2024. This is August 2023. February 2024. So what we're seeing here is that the Russians have really built, as you can see here, munitions storage area, numerous occupied revetted storage areas throughout. So they built new revetments in the storage area that are completely being filled with North Korean ammunition.

Another example of this is Mozdok, a storage facility where we see a lot of activity again starting in the new year because of North Korean munitions. And then this is, I can't pronounce this, but it's an airfield in Russia. This is a picture of it in September 2023, pretty much an abandoned airfield in Russia that is near the war front. with Ukraine. And this is what it looks like in September of 2023. And this is what it looks like in January of 2024. Again, approximately 320 newly constructed storage revetments, many of which are occupied. And so these are all sort of physical manifestations of the level of cooperation that is taking place between North Korea and Russia. The White House has said 10,000 shipping containers of ammunition. The South Korean defense ministry has said over 3 million rounds of ammunition, plus North Korean ballistic missiles have been found landing in Ukraine. So a very deep, very deep, deep relationship.

The most recent manifestation of this cooperation happened at the end of last week where North Korea vetoed a UN Security Council resolution to renew the mandate of the UN Panel of experts. The un panel of Experts is responsible for monitoring compliance with the UN sanctions regime on North Korea. And so I think that this is part of an effort by Russia to completely dismantle the UN sanctions regime against North Korea. The first step in doing this was to no longer comply with the sanctions. Russia is not complying with any of the UN sanctions that it had signed on to previously. Then it has, you know, blocking the renewables of the panel of experts is the second step. And then the third step is they are calling for sunset clauses to the UN sanctions that are contained in the 10 UN Security Council resolutions on North Korea.

What does this all mean for South Korea and the United States? I think there are many things but let me just close with talking about one thing in particular, which is that What they wore in Ukraine has made very clear is that the UN Security Council can no longer be the institution of global governance for the rules-based international order and for like-minded countries in the rules-based international order because China and Russia will basically block any action in the un security council.

The G20 20 is too big a grouping for institutional governments and the BRICS as well are too big and both of them include China. And so increasing, it looks like the only viable institution for global governance is the G7, the Group of Seven, of like-minded partners that can coordinate policy in the absence of the UN acting as a global governance institution. And why this matters for the United States and South Korea is that the G7 as it currently stands is not fit for purpose. It is not ready to take on this mandate as a new institution of global governance for the rules-based international order. And the G7 needs to expand. And by expansion, I mean it needs to include countries like South Korea, Australia, and even other European countries like

Spain in order in order for it to play this role to meet the challenges of global governance now that the Ukraine war and sanctions on North Korea show that the UN can no longer do that.

So, Dr. Jun, let me stop here. And I'm happy to take any questions about what I've discussed or anything else that your colleagues would like to talk about.

Jun Kwang-woo: Okay, thank you very much, Victor, for your brilliant opening remarks, very comprehensive and touching on the very critical issues that we face here on the Korean Peninsula. You made a very clear statement about the increasing provocations from North Korea, which will only get worse in this election year of 2024. And also in dealing with this, in dealing with these challenges, there are some positive developments like the trilateral alliance between the US, Japan and Korea, which is a very important development. But on the other hand, we also have a very important worrying development on North Korea-Russia growing alliance there. And you mentioned some very significant, very serious implications of North Korea's close relationship with Russia.

Now, I would like to move very quickly with discussion. We have two invited guests of discussions. One, let me start with Ambassador Hur Kyung-wook, who is a very prominent government official throughout his career. He was First Vice Minister of Finance and Economy and also served as Korea's Ambassador to OECD, after having career both at the World Bank and IMF. Mr. Hur, The floor is yours.

Hur Kyung-wook: Thank you very much for the excellent presentation. You provided us with a very accurate picture, but at the same time very bleak picture of increasing threat from North Korea. And the problem of discussing North Korea is always you are left with bad option, worse option, or the worst option. And I'm relieved that you substantiated that the view in some corners of the U.S. that Kim Jong Un might have made a strategic decision to go to war that may not be well substantiated, that's relieving.

But at the same time, we have two great concerns. Number one is a domestic issue. Despite all these increasing threats of North Korea and their unholy alliance with Russia, there is a naive view in some corners of Korean society that peace is everything at all costs so that maybe all these increasing threats from North Korea might be triggered by this Camp David declaration, which I don't agree at all, but there's increasing view in some corners of Korean society. That's worrisome. That's number one. I would like to seek your view on that.

Number two is that, you know, you said the G7, expansion of G7, but U.S. presidential election is coming and if Mr. Trump comes back as the president, there is an increasing worry that he basically likes to make a deal. And if he makes a deal with North Korea behind our back, and in that regard, if he decided to pull out or reduce the US Army's presence from Korea, what would be our option? There's a growing voice that it might be high time for Korea to think seriously about developing our own nuclear capacity if that happens how likely it might be and whether do you think the international community can accept the careers uh willingness to develop its own nuclear capacity that's my two questions thank you.

Victor Cha: Thank you, Ambassador Hur, for those very good questions. I will try to answer them concisely given that time is short. First on the Camp David question, whether Camp David is causing this North Korean behavior. That is actually why I started out the presentation by presenting all the data to show very clearly that this North Korean behavior predates, predates, David effort and the improvement in Japan-Korea relations, and that there are very clear reasons why they are doing this. As I said, scientific testing, operational exercising, they're doing these completely irrespective of whether there was Camp David or wasn't it. But I agree there are some who are saying that these two things are linked, but in my mind, they're not, and that there are very complete, there are completely independent drivers for why North Korea is carrying out all this very heightened provocations.

With regard to the question of Trump, I think, you know,

what North Korea will do in 2024 will put whoever wins the White House in 2025 in a position similar to where Donald Trump was in 2017, which is that this will become, in spite of the war in Ukraine and Gaza, this will become the number one issue for the new president. But I think in talking to some of Trump's people in the first term, my sense is that his instinct will not will be to not go back to 2017 fire and fury. That will not be what he'll do. His instinct will be to try to pick up where he left off with Kim Jong Un, with some at the diplomacy.

And there it's possible that he would try to make a deal of sanctions lifting in return for no long-range ballistic missile tests and no nuclear tests, but not denuclearization, not short-range ballistic missiles or things that would be threatening to South Korea. That's decoupling, right? And that sort of decoupling, I think, would raise serious concerns in South Korea and could spark really a national security discussion about what South Korea should do next.

Jun Kwang-woo: Okay, thank you very much. Now, let's move on to our second discussant who is Professor Kim Jin-il. He's at Korea University with graduate degrees from Yale University. He's a truly emerging academic leader in economics in Korea, having extensive experience overseas, such as working at US Federal Reserve, IMF, and Georgetown University as well. So, okay, let's welcome Professor Kim.

Kim Jin-il: Thanks, Dr. Jun. Hello, professor cha. Thank you and good to see you again. Let me pick up the second last question by Ambassador Herr about this election and in one of the two scenarios, probably the more likely you are familiar with the Trump scenario. I'd like to ask about the trade issues. That's more unfamiliar. You told that Trump will pick over his left in terms of diplomacy. But trade is a little more complicated than that, I believe. the four years of the Biden term would affect the trade issues here and there. So what are the issues we should think of? If Trump wins, what would happen to the trade side, especially with China? Because Korea is probably the country that is affected by the most, by China and the United States. So great if we can hear your view on that. Thank you.

Victor Cha: I have a couple of responses. The first is that I think when it comes to allies, I don't think Trump's views would change. In other words, he still views allies as trade adversaries. And I think that any country or any ally that has a trade surplus with the United States, and that would include South Korea, I think that he will put tariffs. he will slap a 10% tariff, for example, across the board. As outrageous as that might sound, it's highly possible that he'll do that. With regard to China, I think it could go in one of two directions.

There are some, and we actually heard this view during the Republican primary by the moderate Republicans, but the moderate Republicans like Nikki Haley, there's a part of the Republican Party that is actually calling for revoking PNTR for China, right? So like really hardline decoupling of trade with China. And in that regard, Trump might actually be more moderate than that because he may focus on sort of very high tariffs as he did in the first term but might not go so far as to call for revoking PNTR for China.

However, at the same time, I think that there will be continuity with the Biden administration on economic security issues. So whether we're talking about chips or AI or quantum computing, I fully expect that a Biden administration will actually continue, a Trump administration, would actually continue what the Biden administration did in large part because I think Donald Trump feels like he started that idea. And in fact, we did see it in the Trump administration, this effort, whether it was on BRI financing or on Huawei 5G to really try to decouple from China. So I think that in that regard, he will still be, the Chinese should not expect to see anything different from a Trump administration as they're seeing with the Biden administration. And they are quite concerned.

The Chinese are quite concerned about what the Biden administration has accomplished thus far with regard to supply chain security in these so-called high fence, small yard areas. But the other thing, again, that makes it so complicated with Trump is that at a personal level, I think he will still try to engage with Xi Jinping. I think he will still try to engage with him at a personal level and try to talk about strategic engagement when at the same time on the economic side, it's going to be a very competitive and difficult relationship.

Jun Kwang-woo: Great, thank you Victor. Now I'm compelled to ask you a couple of questions for the benefit of our members and viewers, if you don't mind.

The first question has to do with the situation in Taiwan. The other day, actually last week as I understand it, there was an important remark, testimony came out of the Capitol Hill where the US Indo-Pacific Commander, Admiral John Aquilino had said that China appears to be moving forward to be prepared to invade Taiwan by 2027. That is one year before Mr. Xi Jinping's third term expires. Now, your quick view of how dangerous the situation is, perhaps, to develop in the coming years that could and must have serious implications for peace on the Korean Peninsula? So that's one question.

The second has to do with our discussions, which have raised the question of the impact of Trump in the upcoming November elections. In this context, how do you see the future of the very important trilateral relationship between the United States, Japan and Korea? If Mr. Trump wins, some might expect that the trilateral relationship might not be as strong as it is under Mr. Biden. So what is your view on that?

And finally, maybe a lot of people are talking about the Trump risk, the kind of risk implications of a Trump victory. But I think when we talk about risk, there's also the other side of the coin, which is, what's good just in case, Mr. Trump wins for the security arrangement in this part of the world. A lot of peole talk about adverse changes and the unpredictable nature of his style. But I'd like to hear some positive notes in case Mr. Trump comes back as a president. Thank you.

Victor Cha: Thank you, Dr. Jun, for those questions. Let me tie at least the last point of opportunity together with your initial comment. So it's possible that one opportunity might be to try to convince Donald Trump that expansion of the G7 to having countries like Korea and Australia in it is something that could be seen for him as sort of his special stamp on the G7. As you remember, he had a very antagonistic relationship with the G7, with Angela Merkel and others. And, you know, and we just complained to the Europeans about how they need to increase defense spending. But if he could be seen as sort of putting his unique stamp on the G7 by expanding it to the G10 with countries like Korea and Australia and Spain, he might actually like that. I mean, anything that he can say that it was him, he might like that.

So I think that's one opportunity. I think the other opportunity is that Trump will not want to spend a lot on defending allies. You'll want to stop the exercising, a lot of these things. But that could also mean opportunities for

Korea. I don't think that there will be, I think there would be hardly any restraints on what Korea wanted to do in terms of their own defense spending and military acquisitions.

On Taiwan, yes, it's very concerning. And, you know, we should take very seriously when the Indo-Pacific commander of the United States says he's concerned that China is getting ready for war in 2027. There are two things that I would note. The first is that I don't think Xi Jinping right now has any confidence in that his military could actually fail. fight a war in the Taiwan Straits. Right now, he's so worried about corruption in his military, and he does not believe it's a fighting force.

It is a vehicle for graft and corruption, but it's not a fighting force. And I don't think he's comfortable at all that they're ready for something like that. And that he's seen sort of the sort of casualties we're seeing in the war in Ukraine. And we have to remember, like China, the Chinese people, the Chinese government, the Chinese military, they have not seen casualties in war since what the Korean War. They have not seen casualties in war. And a Taiwan fight would be extremely bloody. We know that. And there will be major losses for the Chinese. The second, the only thing that would make me more concerned is that, as you know well, we have a new government in Taiwan coming in May. And people, we really don't have a good sense of William Lai. the president-elect. He's not very focused on foreign policy issues. He's not very strong on cross-strait relations.

And we know he has sort of a nativist nationalist instinct. So if he's the variable that all of a sudden says something very provocative, then Xi Jinping will have no choice. but to do something. But that's where the United States, I think, has to play a role in ensuring that that sort of scenario doesn't come to pass.

Jun Kwang-woo: Okay, great. Thank you very much, Victor, for your brilliant speech and stimulating discussion afterwards. Thank you very much once again, and I hope to have you in person next time around here in Seoul. Wish you all the best. I look forward to seeing you soon. thank you.

Victor Cha: Thank you

미국 대선 이후 무역정책 변화와 중국 및 한국 경제에 미치는 영향 분석

제프리 샷
(Jeffrey J. Schott)

제프리 샷

Jeffrey J. Schott

   국제 무역 정책과 경제 제재를 연구하는 피터슨국제경제연구소의 Senior Fellow이다. 카네기 국제평화재단의 수석연구원과 미국 재무부의 국제무역 및 에너지정책 관리를 역임했다. 또한 국무부의 대외경제정책 자문위원회의 위원이었으며 미국 무역대표부 무역 및 환경 정책 자문위원회의 공동의장으로 활동했다.

[2024년 10월 16일]

미국 대선 이후 무역정책 변화와 중국 및 한국 경제에 미치는 영향 분석

제프리 샷
미 조지타운대학교 석좌교수
미국 피터슨 국제경제연구소(PIIE) Senior Fellow

전광우 이사장: 안녕하십니까, IGE 웨비나 포럼에 오신 것을 환영합니다. 미국 대통령 선거가 이제 불과 3주 앞으로 다가온 만큼 오늘 웨비나에서는 국제 무역 정책 분야의 세계적 권위자인 제프리 샷 박사를 연사로 모시고, 미 대선 관련 매우 시의 적절한 국제 무역 현안들과 새로운 쟁점에 대해 심도 있는 논의를 진행하고자 합니다. 새롭게 들어설 미국 행정부에서 변화가 예상되는 무역 정책들의 의미와 아시아, 특히 중국과 한국에 미치는 영향과 시사점에 대해서도 살펴볼 예정입니다.

제프리 샷 박사님은 현재 피터슨국제경제연구소(PIIE)에서 국제 무역 정책과 경제 제재를 연구하는 Senior Fellow로 재직 중입니다. 미국 재무부에서 국제 무역 및 에너지 정책을 담당하였으며 2003년부터는 미국 국무부 국제경제정책 자문위원회 위원으로 활동하고 있습니다.

오늘은 저희 웨비나를 위해 늦은 시간에도 불구하고 미국 플로리다 현지에서 생방송으로 함께하고 계십니다. 그럼 이제 제프리 샷 박사님을 모시겠습니다. 박사님 안녕하세요?

제프리 샷 박사: 안녕하세요. 친절한 소개 감사드립니다. 오늘 세계경제연구원 웨비나에 함께하게 되어 매우 기쁩니다. 그럼 바로 본론으로 들어가겠습니다.

미국 대선이 불과 3주 앞으로 다가왔고 이미 사전 투표가 진행되고 있지만 모든 여론 조사에서 공화당 트럼프 후보와 민주당 해리스 후보가 박빙의 승부를 펼치고 있기 때문에 이번 선거에서 누가 당선될지 현재로서는 예측하기가 매우 어려운 상황입니다. 다만, 이번 선거가 향후 미국 경제 정책 방향에 큰 변화를 가져올 것이라는 점은 확실하며 저는 이점에 대해 매우 우려하고 있습니다.

Growing challenges to postwar global economic relations

- Postwar progress at risk of unraveling as cold trade wars, hot wars, and new waves of protectionism masked by patriotic fervor threaten to disrupt/constrain international trade and investment.
- US-China cold trade war since 2018, with tit-for-tat trade retaliation and investment restrictions, in a downward spiral.
- Hot wars in Ukraine and Middle East could spread; already threaten vital economic infrastructure (oil/gas pipelines/terminals; transport on Black Sea and via Suez Canal/Red Sea).
- Growing use of national security exceptions, and disregard for WTO obligations, undercutting support for rules-based trading system.
- Near-term outlook darkens depending on who is in the White House after January 20, 2025.

Schott, US Post-Election Trade Policy Outlook

지난 50년 동안 저는 보조금에 관한 세계 무역 규칙을 만들고, 국제에너지기구가 2차 오일쇼크에서 석유 카르텔에 맞서도록 돕고, 북미 경제 통합을 촉진하고, 태평양 건너 한-미 FTA와 환태평양경제동반자협정을 통해 국제 경제 질서를 구축하는 데 노력했으며, 정책 입안자들에게 경제 제재의 오남용을 경계하도록 경고해왔습니다. 우리는 많은 진전을 이루었습니다. 1960년대 세계에서 가장 가난한 경제국가 중 하나였던 한국은 산업 강국이 된 위대한 진전을 이루었습니다. 이는 많은 사람들의 노력과 수고 덕분입니다.

하지만 애국적 열정으로 포장된 새로운 냉전과 무력 전쟁(hot wars), 새로운 보호무역주의의 물결이 국제 무역과 투자를 방해하거나 제약할 위협을 가하면서 전후 시대에 우리가 이룩한 많은 진전이 무너지고 있는 것은 아닌지 우려됩니다. 2018년부터 미중 무역 전쟁이 계속되고 있습니다. 중국산 수입품에 대한 미국의 대규모 관세 부과와 미국산 상품과 서비스, 투자에 대한 중국의 무역 보복이 이어졌습니다. 미중 무역 경제 관계는 제한과 맞대응의 소용돌이 속에 갇혀 있는 것처럼 보입니다.

동시에 우크라이나와 중동에서는 무력 전쟁이 확산될 위험에 처해 있습니다. 이미 후티 반군이 홍해를 통과하는 선박을 폭격하면서 이 지역의 중요한 경제 인프라, 석유 및 가스 파이프라인과 터미널이 위협받고 있고, 흑해와 수에즈 운하 및 홍해를 통한 운송이 중단되고 있습니다. 이는 유럽과 아시아 간 무역 네트워크를 단축하고 개선하기 위해 수에즈 운하를 이용해온 많은 국가의 무역에 영향을 미칩니다.

국가 안보 예외를 악용하고 WTO 의무를 무시하는 사례도 증가하고 있습니다. 이는 규칙에 기반한 다자간 무역 시스템에 대한 지지를 약화시키고 있습니다. 제네바에서 협상이 진행 중이지만 결과는 매우 희박하고 산발적입니다. 기후와 디지털 무역과 같은 중요한 문제에 대한 WTO의 역할을 회복시키려는 노력은 아무 진전이 없는 것 같습니다. 이로 인해 양자 및 지역적 수단을 통해 무역 시스템을 강화하는 방안을 모색하는 노력으로 이어졌습니다. 이에 대해서는 잠시 후에 말씀드리겠습니다.

2025년 1월 20일 누가 백악관에 입성하느냐에 따라 단기 전망은 어두워질 수 있습니다. 그래서 저는 미국 정책이 직면한 몇 가지 과제와 트럼프 대통령과 해리스 부통령이 이러한 문제를 다룰 때 취할 수 있는 다양한 접근 방식에 대해 설명하고자 합니다.

Big differences between Trump/Harris on approach to key issues on 2025 US economic agenda

- Revising/extending 2017 tax cuts.
- Rebuilding US military and reinforcing industries vital to national security.
- Confronting Chinese competition at home and abroad via new tariffs, nontariff barriers affecting Chinese trade/FDI, and export controls blunting tech transfer to Chinese firms.
- Preparing for USMCA 6-year review (conflicts over autos, energy, agriculture, Mexican judicial reforms).
- Confronting Russian aggression via economic/military support for Ukraine and tighter economic sanctions (affecting global oil markets).

Schott, US Post-Election Trade Policy Outlook

먼저 2025년 미국의 경제 의제입니다. 국제적으로 큰 반향을 일으킬 이슈는 아니지만 미국 국내 및 대외 경제 정책에 큰 영향을 미칠 사안들입니다. 무엇보다도 도널드 트럼프 1기 행정부 출범 첫해에 통과되어 2025년 말 만료될 예정인 2017 감세 정책을 수정하거나 연장하려는 노력이 가장 먼저 이루어질 것으로 예상

됩니다(대부분 내년 말까지 만료될 예정). 트럼프는 감세가 경제 성장을 촉진하고 그 자체로 효과를 거둘 것이라고 생각하여 일부 감세를 연장하고 더 심화하기를 원할 것 입니다. 다만 과거에도 그런 일이 거의 없었고 경제학계에서는 앞으로도 그러한 효과를 기대할 만한 증거가 없다며 회의적인 입장입니다. 해리스 부통령은 미국 사회의 소외계층을 위한 사회 프로그램에 더 많은 세수를 투입하기 위해 특히 부유층과 중상류층에 혜택을 주는 감세 정책을 축소하고자 합니다. 물론 시간이 걸리겠지만요. 2025년에는 의회의 추가적인 노력과 행동이 필요할 수 있는데, 이는 11월에 있을 대통령 선거처럼 의회 역시 민주당과 공화당으로 양분될 것으로 보이기 때문입니다. 어느 정당이 상원을 장악할지, 어느 정당이 하원을 장악할지, 현재로서는 불투명하지만 과반을 넘어 의회를 완전히 장악하기 보다는 근소하게 과반을 넘기며 팽팽하게 맞설 것으로 예상됩니다.

미군을 재건하고 국가 안보에 필수적인 산업을 강화해야 하는 과제도 남아 있습니다. 그 중 일부는 인플레이션 억제법의 결과이며 미국 반도체 산업의 재건과 업그레이드에 초점을 맞추고 있습니다. 그러나 미군 시설과 인력뿐만 아니라 특히 함정 등의 장비를 업그레이드해야 할 필요성도 있습니다. 중동과 아시아에서 벌어지고 있는 첨예하고 위협적인 적대 행위의 특성을 고려할 때 미국은 실제로 더 많은 군함이 필요합니다. 그러기 위해서는 동맹국의 도움이 필요하지만 많은 비용이 소요될 것입니다. 따라서 감세와 군사 및 산업 개발에 더 많은 지출을 해야 합니다.

중국과의 경쟁을 위한 새로운 관세 부과는 트럼프, 해리스 두 후보 모두 추진할 것이라고 생각합니다. 그리고 여기에는 중국 무역과 FDI에 영향을 미치는 비관세 장벽도 포함될 것입니다. 특히 미국의 수출 통제, 중국 기업에 대한 기술 이전 억제, 미국, 한국, 일본 정책의 긴밀한 조율이 필요할 것입니다. 내년에는 또한 미국이 미국-멕시코-캐나다 협정의 6년 의무 검토 준비를 시작해야하는데, 자동차, 에너지, 농업을 둘러싼 갈등과 최근 멕시코에서 제정된 사법 개혁이 북미 3국 간의 새로운 논란과 갈등을 야기하고 통합 협정에 큰 마찰을 초래할 수 있습니다. 실제로 도널드 트럼프의 위협은 멕시코를 니어쇼어링의 거점으로 삼으려는 미국의 힘을 사용할 수 있는 능력을 약화시킬 수도 있습니다. 동아시아에서 북미로 생산기지를 옮기고 멕시코 시설에서 미국으로 운송할 투자 기회를 찾는다면 니어쇼어링을 고려해야합니다.

마지막으로, 러시아의 침략에 맞서려면 우크라이나에 대한 경제 및 군사 지원이 필요하며 세계 석유 시장에 영향을 미치는 경제 제재를 강화해야 합니다. 이는 두 후보가 매우 큰 차이를 보이는 분야이며 세계 경제와 세계 평화에 매우 중대한 영향을 미칠 수 있는 사안입니다. 솔직히 트럼프는 우크라이나 경제와 군사 보호를 위해 쓰여져야 할 자금을 줄이기 위해 미국의 국익을 위한다는 명목으로 블라디미르 푸틴과 기꺼이 거래를 할 의향이 있는 것 같습니다. 해리스 부통령은 우크라이나에 대한 지원을 계속할 것이지만, 석유 시장에 지금까지보다 훨씬 더 큰 타격을 줄 수 있는 미국의 경제 제재를 강화하고 확대할지 여부를 결정해야 하는 어려운 과제에 직면하게 될 것입니다.

본질적으로 푸틴 대통령은 세계 시장에서 석유를 계속 판매할 수 있었기 때문에 러시아 경제에 대한 실질적인 피해에 대해 면죄부를 받았습니다. 그리고 이를 통해 연간 수천억 달러의 수입을 벌어들여 러시아 경제를 많은 왜곡이 있지만 전쟁을 계속할 수 있는 전쟁 중심 경제로 전환할 수 있었습니다. 석유를 제한하기 위해 이러한 제재를 강화하면 국제 유가에 큰 영향을 미쳐 푸틴 대통령에게 영향을 미칠 것이 분명하지만, 서방 국가와 동아시아 소비자들의 비용도 상승할 것입니다. 이 모든 것이 의미하는 바는 제 책 '무역 정책에 대한 심층 분석'의 서문에서 언급했듯이 차기 미국 대통령이 이 모든 상황에 어떻게 대응하느냐에 따라 중요한 결과를 초래할 수 있다는 것입니다.

> **Key consequences of domestic and international economic decisions in 2025**
>
> - 2025 priorities will require additional federal revenues and cuts to some programs/benefits, including possibly IRA, Chips and Science Act.
> - Changes to US tax policies, additional military expenditures, trade and investment interventions, and primary/secondary economic sanctions:
>   - exacerbate funding challenges and/or
>   - risk spiking inflationary pressures via burgeoning budget deficits and protection-induced price increases.
> - Markets will recognize the obvious before politicians and interest rates will rise.

그런데 중요한 것은 누가 당선이 되든 이와 같은 주요 경제 의제를 위해서는 추가적인 연방 세입이 필요하다는 것입니다. 아마도 인플레이션 감축법(IRA) 및 반도체 과학법(CHIPS)을 포함한 일부 프로그램과 혜택에 대한 삭감이 필요할 것입니다. 도널드 트럼프 당선시에는 더욱 그러할 가능성이 더 높습니다. 트럼프는 미국의 세금 정책 변경, 추가 군사비 지출, 무역 및 투자 개입, 1차 및 2차 경제 제재에 따른 예산 수입이 감세에 따른 세입 감소를 충당할 수 있기를 원합니다.

이로 인해 시장에 어떤 일이 일어날지 살펴보면, 미국 정부의 재정 문제를 악화시켜 예산 적자 급증과 보호무역으로 인한 가격 인상으로 인플레이션 압력이 급증할 것이 분명합니다. 많은 상품에 관세를 부과하면 결국 그 부담은 미국 소비자들에게 전이될 것입니다. 수입품에 의존하는 개인 가정과 기업 모두의 비용이 증가할 것입니다. 트럼프의 계획은 향후 10년 동안 미국의 재정 적자를 3조~4조 달러까지 늘릴 것으로 추정되지만, 그는 관세가 많은 추가 수입을 올릴 것이라고 말하며 이를 가볍게 일축합니다. 관세 인상이 더 큰 예산 적자를 초래하지 않고 미국 경제를 더 강하게 만들 것이라는 그의 환상을 제외하면 그런 결론에 도달할 수 있는 경험적 수학적 근거는 없습니다. 시장은 정치인의 포부보다는 명백한 사실에 반응할 것이기 때문에 금리가 상승할 것입니다. 그리고 이는 내년 미국 경제 성장을 둔화 시키고 미국의 무역 역량과 무역 규모에 영향을 미칠 것입니다.

> **Implications for US Trade Policy in 2025**
>
> - US trade policy will be inward-looking more than internationalist.
> - Domestic politics will increase pressure for migration controls, and negatively impact labor markets beyond the border and across farm, industry, and services sectors.
> - National security restrictions on steel/aluminum/other tech products will continue; so, too, will China trade war tariffs.
> - Export controls against China/Russia/Iran/North Korea on sensitive technologies will broaden/deepen.
> - Anti-China trade/investment policies will be extended to constrain or decouple the two economies. Chinese export expansion via third countries will provoke US to pressure Korea, Mexico, ASEAN to limit ties with China... putting Korea (and Japan) between a rock and a hard place.

이제 2025년 미국 무역 정책에 대한 시사점에 대해 살펴보겠습니다. 모두가 제가 이 부분부터 시작할 것이라고 생각했지만, 앞으로 일어날 많은 일들이 예산 경색의 영향을 받을 것이라는 점을 인식해야 한다고 생각해서 이 부분을 두번째로 말씀드리게 되었습니다. 그렇다면 미국의 무역 정책이 예산 경색을 개선하게 될까요, 아니면 악화시키게 될까요? 대부분의 측면에서 저는 무역 정책이 상황을 더욱 악화시킬 것이라고 생각합니다. 트럼프든 해리스든 미국의 무역 정책은 국제주의적이기 보다는 내실을 중시할 것이 분명한데, 이는 해리스보다는 트럼프 당선의 경우가 훨씬 심할 것으로 보입니다.

한편 국내 정치는 이민 통제에 대한 압력을 높일 것입니다. 이는 특히 미국 남서부 지역과 11월 대선에서 누가 승리할지를 부분적으로 결정할 국경 접경 주(州)에서 뜨거운 정치적 이슈가 되고 있습니다. 철강과 알루미늄 및 기타 기술 제품에 대한 국가 안보 제한은 계속될 것입니다. 중국과의 무역 전쟁 관세도 마찬가지입니다. 중국, 러시아, 이란, 북한에 대한 민감한 기술에 대한 수출 통제는 두 후보 중 누가 당선이 되든 더 확대되고 심화될 것입니다. 트럼프가 당선될 경우 러시아 보다 중국에 더 초점을 맞추겠지만 반중 무역 및 투자 정책이 확대되어 두 경제를 제약하거나 분리할 것입니다. 우리는 이미 바이든 대통령이 트럼프의 반중 관세 및 제한 조치를 지속하면서 이런 일이 벌어지는 것을 목격했으며, 이는 제3국을 통한 중국의 수출 확대로 이어졌습니다. 따라서 결국 미국이 아세안 회원국인 한국과 멕시코 같은 국가에 중국과의 관계를 제한하도록 압력을 가하게 될 것인데, 문제는 이들 국가 중 상당수에게 중국은 미국보다 더 큰 무역 파트너라는 점입니다. 따라서 이들 국가들을 진퇴양난에 빠뜨릴 것입니다.

If Trump returns to the White House, Part 1

- Quickly act on campaign pledge to raise all US tariffs by 10% plus an additional 50% on Chinese goods, using national security/emergency powers under Section 232 and IEEPA.
- Across-the-board tariffs could be challenged in court; tariff increases might then initially target China and national security sectors such as steel/aluminum... and autos!
- Tariffs on China will prompt retaliation against US exports and anti-circumvention via transshipment and sourcing from overseas Chinese owned factories in SE Asia and Latin America.
- US neglect/violation of WTO obligations, and withdrawal from WTO also possible; Trump likely to dump IPEF as Biden initiative.

그렇다면 트럼프가 백악관으로 복귀하거나 해리스가 대통령에 당선되면 무역 정책은 어떻게 될까요?

트럼프 당선의 경우부터 생각해보겠습니다. 그는 머릿속에서 떠오르는 대로 많은 말을 하기 때문에, 그가 얼마나 많은 일을 할 것인지, 심지어 하고 싶어할 것인지는 미지수입니다. 하지만 점점 더 관세가 그의 경제 의제의 핵심이고 이민 통제가 그의 정치적 의제의 핵심인 것처럼 보입니다. 따라서 저는 그가 모든 미국산 제품에 대한 관세를 10% 인상하고, 232조와 국제 긴급 경제 권한법에 따라 국가 안보 및 긴급 권한을 사용하여 중국산 제품에 추가로 50%를 인상하겠다는 선거 공약을 신속하게 실행에 옮길 것이라고 생각합니다.

단, 이러한 긴급 권한이 실제로 상업적 정당성이 있는 전반적인 관세에 대해 사용될 수 있는지에 대한 법적 논란이 있습니다. 따라서 법정에서 다툼이 있을 수 있습니다. 그렇다면 적어도 단기적으로는 초기 관세 인상은 알루미늄과 철강, 자동차 등 중국과 국가 안보 부문을 겨냥할 수 있습니다. 자동차 부문이 어떻게 국가 안보 문제냐고 말할 수 있습니다. 철강과 알루미늄에 대해서도 같은 지적을 할 수 있습니다. 이에 대해서는 잠시 후에 트럼프의 관점에서 답을 드리겠습니다.

또 다른 중요한 요점은 트럼프가 대통령이 사용할 수 있는 기존 권한으로 1950년대 초 아이젠하워 행정부에서 발생한 것보다 더 크지는 않더라도 100만 명 이상의 근로자에게 영향을 미칠 수 있는 대규모 이민자 추방을 요청하고 제정할 수 있다는 것입니다. 이러한 강제 추방 또는 체포와 추방 과정은 미국 노동 공급에 큰 부정적 충격을 주어 인플레이션을 높이고 생산량을 감소시킬 것입니다. 스태그플레이션을 의미합니다. 그 결과 트럼프가 예측한 것과는 정반대로 GDP가 감소하고 내구성 있는 제조업 일자리가 감소할 것입니다. 이민 정책의 노동 시장을 통한 이러한 충격은 추가 관세로 인한 초기 관세 충격보다 훨씬 더 클 수 있습니다. 그래서 이는 정말 심각하게 살펴볼 필요가 있습니다.

중국에 대한 관세는 미국 수출에 대한 보복과 동남아시아와 라틴 아메리카의 화교 공장에서의 환적 및 소싱을 통한 우회 반발을 촉발할 것입니다. 이는 바이든이 이미 멕시코에 가한 것처럼 중국으로부터의 상품 수입 및 투자 심사에 관한 정책을 재검토하라는 압력으로 이어질 것입니다. 그런데 이들 국가는 중국 내륙에서 베트남이나 말레이시아, 멕시코 또는 라틴 아메리카의 다른 지역으로 중국 생산을 이전함으로써 큰 이익을 얻습니다. 따라서 우호적인 무역 파트너들이 중국과 더 많은 거래를 하지 못하도록 강요하는 것뿐만 아니라 멕시코와 말레이시아, 베트남 등 우방국 상품의 미국 시장 진입을 제한하는 등의 강압을 시행하기 시작하면 몇 가지 심각한 문제가 있을 것입니다. 과거에 트럼프는 미국의 우방과 동맹국에 대해 철강과 알루미늄에 관세를 부과한 적이 있는데, 무역전쟁 관세를 회피하려는 중국의 노력을 무력화하기 위해 다시 그렇게 할 수 있습니다.

세계 무역 규칙을 준수하는 것은 어떨까요? 글쎄요, 그것은 이전에 트럼프를 멈춘 적이 없습니다. 그리고 2017년 초 트럼프가 환태평양경제동반자협정(TPP)에서 했던 것처럼 미국의 WTO 의무 무시와 위반이 계속될 것이며, 심지어는 WTO 자체에서 탈퇴할 가능성도 있습니다. 트럼프는 또한 인도 태평양 경제 체제 이니셔티브가 바이든의 이니셔티브이고 그와 연관되기를 원하지 않기 때문에 이를 포기할 가능성이 높습니다.

> **If Trump returns to the White House, Part 2**
>
> - Focus on US trade deficit with Korea, especially in autos:
>   - US merchandise deficit running at annual rate of almost $60 billion so far this year;
>   - Deficit in the auto sector more than $43 billion annualized.
> - Trump could threaten to disrupt KORUS FTA like he did with NAFTA unless Korea changes policies to meet US demands (e.g., regarding defense burden-sharing, FDI in US in autos/semiconductors, export controls).
> - Climate policies will be downgraded/IRA subsidies and other climate incentives not supported by Big Oil/Big 3 automakers reduced or defunded.
> - Possible support for US CBAM, not for climate purposes but to generate tariff revenues from carbon-intensive imports.

하지만 트럼프가 할 수 있는 일은 더 있습니다. 첫째는 미국의 대 한국 무역 적자, 특히 자동차에 대한 집중입니다. 이것은 트럼프가 항상 집중하고 있는 부분입니다. 그리고 미국의 대 한국 무역, 상품 무역 적자 증가는 그의 관심을 끌기에 매우 매력적인 대상입니다. 올해 미국의 상품수지 적자가 연간 600억 달러 수준에 육박하고 있는데 한국과의 자동차 부문 적자가 430억 달러가 넘습니다. 그래서 한국과의 적자와 그것이 어떻게 집중되어 있는지에 초점을 맞추면 트럼프가 미국 경제 보호를 명목으로 자동차에 새로운 관세를 부과할 수 있다는 결론에 도달할 수 있습니다. 이제 트럼프는 한국이 미국의 요구에 맞게 정책을 바꾸지 않으면 NAFTA에서 그랬던 것처럼 한미 FTA를 파기하겠다고 위협할 수 있습니다. 방위비 부담, 자동차 및 반도체에 대한 미국의 외국인 직접 투자, 수출 통제에 관한 미국 정책과의 연계 등을 요구하고 있습니다. 트럼프가 즐겨 사용하는 경제적 강압의 영역은 시진핑과 어떤 면에서는 매우 유사합니다.

트럼프가 대통령이 되면 기후 정책은 하향 조정될 것입니다. 대형 석유회사나 빅3 자동차 제조업체가 지원하지 않는 일부 IRA 보조금과 기타 기후 인센티브가 삭감될 수 있으며, 이러한 보조금은 축소되거나 자금이 환수될 수 있습니다. 그런데 트럼프가 친기후적인 것처럼 보이는 행동을 할 수 있는 한가지 영역이 있긴 합니다. 그는 미국의 탄소 국경 조정 메커니즘 조치, 즉 본질적으로 기후 목적이 아니라 탄소 집약적 수입, 철강 타격, 알루미늄 타격, 탄소 발자국이 큰 다른 제품 타격에서 추가 수입을 창출하기 위해 새로운 탄소 관세를 지지할 수 있습니다.

아직 환율 정책에 대해서는 언급하지 않았는데요, 환율 정책은 국제 무역과 투자에 영향을 미칠 수 있는 트럼프 경제 프로그램의 중요한 부분이기도 합니다. 트럼프는 달러 약세를 원합니다. 그는 달러 약세가 미국의 수출을 장려하고 미국을 보완할 것이라고 생각합니다. 하지만, 미국 시장을 보호하기 위해 관세를 부과는 등 그가 추진하는 정책은 기본적으로 재정 적자를 급증시킬 것이기 때문에 금리를 인상할 것이고, 금리가 올라가면 중기적으로 달러 가치를 끌어올리는 효과를 가져와 트럼프가 원하는 것과는 정반대의 결과를 가져올 것입니다. 이는 트럼프가 집권할 경우 미국 경제에 대한 광범위한 문제이지만 무역 정책에도 중요한 영향을 미칩니다.

> **US Trade Policy Priorities under Kamala Harris**
>
> - Compared to Trump, Harris would treat friends/allies more like friends and allies:
>   - Strengthen US-Korea collaboration on semiconductors;
>   - Increased reliance on Korean shipbuilding to support both commercial transport and defense;
>   - Coordinate on economic security policies, sanctions and export controls, with Korea and Japan.
>   - Closer cooperation on climate policies/carbon mitigation.
> - Unlike Trump, more focus on climate/trade nexus, including on plurilateral initiatives, and less overt threat to change KORUS FTA.
> - But would maintain China-specific trade restrictions/investment controls.
> - Continue IPEF initiatives under pillar 2 (supply chain resilience) and pillar 3 (climate projects).

해리스가 당선되면 무역 정책의 우선순위를 정하는 데 더 많은 시간을 할애할 수 있습니다. 현 정부의 정책 기반에서 출발하기 때문입니다. 하지만 트럼프와 비교했을 때 해리스는 중요한 면에서 그 정책을 완화할 것입니다. 트럼프에 비해 해리스는 우방과 동맹국을 더 우방과 동맹국답게 대할 것입니다. 그리고 이것은 반도체에 대한 미-한 협력을 더욱 강화할 수 있습니다. 저는 이것이 매우 중요하다고 생각합니다.

그녀는 강력하고 역동적인 첨단 산업과 첨단 연구 개발 역량을 갖추는 것이 중요하다는 것을 잘 알고 있습니다. 따라서 해리스 행정부가 우선적으로 투자해야 할 분야가 될 것입니다. 또한 미국이 상업 수송과 방위를 모두 지원하기 위해 한국 조선업에 대한 의존도가 높아지고 있다는 점도 잘 알고 있을 것입니다. 이에 미국과 한국의 선박 방어 체계가 훨씬 더 광범위하게 동맹과 연계를 맺고, 우리의 해운 역량을 재건하는 데 있어 한국에 더 많이 의존하게 될 것이라고 생각합니다. 경제 안보 정책, 제재 및 수출 통제에 대해 더 긴밀하게 조율할 것입니다.

제재 정책에 대해서는 자세히 언급하지 않았지만, 서방 국가들의 중국 및 러시아와의 무역 및 투자에 영향을 미치거나 부수적인 피해를 줄 수 있는 금융 기관에 대해 보다 엄격하고 침입적인 2차 제재를 부과하려고 하는데, 이는 미국이 러시아와 중국과의 적대 관계와 관련된 또 다른 도화선이 될 수 있습니다. 해리스와 트럼프의 가장 큰 차이점은 트럼프와 달리 해리스는 다자간 이니셔티브를 포함한 기후 무역 넥서스에 더 초점을 맞추고 FTA의 진로를 바꾸려는 노골적인 위협이 적다는 점입니다.

저는 해리스가 기후 이니셔티브의 강력한 지지자라고 생각합니다. 그녀가 미국-멕시코-캐나다 협정에 반대표를 던진 이유는 기후변화라는 단어가 언급되지 않은 환경 부분이 매우 약했기 때문입니다. 따라서 그녀는 무역과 기후 문제를 연계하는 데 훨씬 더 집중하고 탄소 감축과 재생 가능 기술의 발전을 위한 효과적인 프로그램을 개발하기 위해 최근 몇 년 동안 미국보다 더 많은 조치를 취하고 있는 국가들과 더 긴밀히 협력하려고 노력할 것이라고 생각합니다.

중국에 대한 무역 제한과 투자 통제는 유지할 것입니다. 또한 공급망 회복력, 기후, 프로젝트 관련 인도 태평양 이니셔티브도 계속 추진할 것입니다. 이 두 분야는 미국과 한국이 매우 긴밀하게 협력해 온 분야이며, IPEF가 실제로 양국 간 협력을 위한 추가 영역을 제공하고 있는 분야입니다. 그러나 해리스가 WTO 개정이나 업그레이드에 더 우선순위를 둘 것이라는 징후는 보이지 않습니다. 따라서 현재 WTO의 표류는 계속될 수 있지만 그녀가 조직을 방해하는 데까지 가지는 않을 것이라고 생각합니다. 필요한 만큼의 진전도 없을 것입니다.

> **Policy Implications for Korea**
>
> - Prepare for the extension and possible deepening of the US-China trade war, with concomitant pressure to align with US export controls.
> - Don't expect the KORUS FTA to protect/shield Korean interests from new protectionist measures (including higher auto tariffs), if Trump returns to power. Didn't help with 232 steel tariffs.
> - US commitment to the multilateral trading system will be tepid at best (Harris) and negligible under Trump, who could withdraw from the WTO like he did from the TPP.
> - To reinforce the rules-based trading system, Korea should work more closely with other mid-sized powers to upgrade and expand trade rules promoting economic growth. Participation in the CPTPP as it expands its membership/substantive coverage should be a high priority!
>
> Schott, US Post-Election Trade Policy Outlook

마지막으로 한국에 대한 정책적 시사점을 말씀드리고 마무리하겠습니다. 한국은 미중 무역 전쟁의 장기화 및 심화 가능성과 함께 미국의 수출 규제에 따른 압박에 대비해야 한다고 생각합니다. 트럼프 정부 하에서는 더 강압적일 것이라고 생각합니다. 한미 FTA가 트럼프의 자동차 관세 인상을 포함한 새로운 보호무역 조치로부터 한국의 이익을 보호하고 방어할 것이라고 기대해서는 안됩니다.

트럼프 1기 행정부 당시 232 철강 관세는 도움이되지 않았고 그가 다시 대통령이 되더라도 도움이되지 않을 것입니다. 방금 말씀드린 것처럼 다자 무역 시스템에 대한 미국의 약속은 기껏해야 미지근할 것입니다. 트럼프 하에서는 무시될 수 있습니다. 마지막으로, 규칙 기반 무역 시스템을 강화하기 위해 한국은 더 많은 다른 중견 강대국과 더욱 긴밀히 협력해야 합니다. 이를 통해 무역과 투자를 촉진하고 경제 성장을 촉진하기 위해 양자, 지역 및 WTO에서 무역 규칙을 업그레이드하고 확장해야합니다.

이를 위한 중요한 방법 중 하나는 포괄적·점진적 환태평양 경제 동반자 협정(CPTPP)에 참여하는 것입니다. 현재 이 협정은 첫 5년간의 협정 운영에 대한 검토를 진행하고 있으며, 회원국 확대를 계획하고 있습니다. 그리고 실질적인 적용 범위를 확대하여 한국이 가입하기에 훨씬 더 매력적인 통합 협정이 될 것입니다. 저는 협정이 처음 만들어졌을 때 한국이 가입했어야 한다고 주장해왔지만, 좋은 기회를 활용하기에 아직 늦지 않았다고 생각합니다. 특히, 트럼프가 당선된다면 한국은 당장 CPTPP 가입을 신청해야 합니다. 이는 트럼프 행정부의 정책 남용에 대한 큰 방어책이 될 것이기 때문입니다.

이상으로 발표를 마치겠습니다. 감사합니다.

전광우 이사장: 인사이트가 넘치는 훌륭한 강연을 해 주셔서 대단히 감사합니다. 오늘은 토론자로 이화여자대학교 명예교수이신 유장희 박사님을 모셨습니다. 통상 관련 한국의 가장 저명하고 존경받는 경제학자 중 한 분이십니다. 대외경제정책연구원 원장, 국민경제자문회의 부의장, 동반성장위원회 위원장 등 여러 주요 직책을 역임하신 바 있습니다. 박사님, 함께 해주셔서 감사합니다.

유장희 박사: 안녕하세요 이사장님, 이 중요한 자리에 초대해

주셔서 감사합니다. 그리고 제프리 샷 박사님, 안녕하세요. 다시 만나 뵙게 되어 정말 반갑습니다. 강연 잘 들었습니다.

저는 오늘 강연 내용에서는 다루지 않았던 APEC 정상회의에 관해 논의해 보고자 합니다. APEC 정상회의가 올해 페루에서 열리고 내년(2025년)에는 한국 경주에서 열릴 예정입니다. 미국과 중국 모두 APEC의 주요 회원국이기 때문에 미국 대선 직후인 올해 11월 페루에서 미국 정상과 중국 정상이 만나게 될 것으로 보입니다. 그리고 내년에는 경주에서 만나게 될 것입니다. 그렇게 되면 두 정상이 서로 대화하고 특히 무역 정책을 다루는 데 있어서 서로를 더 잘 이해하려고 노력할 수 있는 좋은 기회를 가질 수 있을 것이라고 확신합니다. 박사님께서는 올해와 내년 APEC 정상회의에 대해 어떤 기대를 하고 계신가요?

제프리 샷 박사: 전 세계적으로 무역 전쟁과 무역 긴장으로 인해 우리가 직면한 문제 중 하나는 신뢰의 부족이기 때문에 매우 좋은 지적입니다. 그리고 사람과 사람 사이의 만남과 관계가 없다면 국내 정치에서 쌓인 불신을 극복하기는 매우 어렵습니다. 그래서 저는 항상 어려운 시기를 겪고 있을 때에도 소통의 채널을 유지하는 것이 매우 중요하다고 생각했습니다. 상대방이 우리의 의도를 잘못 해석하고 오해하고 오판하는 일은 없어야 합니다. APEC 정상회의는 매우 귀중한 회의가 될 것입니다. 미국과 중국이 더 긴밀히 협력할 수 있는 분야가 있고, 특히 다른 APEC 국가들의 지원을 통해 이익을 얻을 수 있는 분야가 있다고 생각합니다.

기후변화 분야는 우리가 공통의 목적을 가지고 있는 분야로, 한국과 일본을 비롯한 다른 국가들이 보다 균형 잡힌 논의와 새로운 이니셔티브에 기여할 수 있는 분야가 될 수 있습니다. 전 세계적으로 미국과 중국이 기후 탄소 감축 협정에 참여하지 않으면 효과적인 결과를 얻을 수 없습니다. APEC에서 진전이 있기를 바랍니다.

CPTPP에서도 그런 일이 일어날 수 있을까요? CPTPP 회원국들이 실질적 적용 범위를 확대하려는 분야 중 하나가 무역과 기후를 다루는 분야라고 생각합니다. 그리고 회원국, 협정 가입을 원하는 국가, 그리고 미국과 유럽연합과 같은 중요한 외부 국가를 초청할 수 있다면 CPTPP에서도 다자간 협정을 체결할 수 있는 토대가 마련될 수 있을 것입니다.

유장희 박사: 중국이 CPTPP에 초대될 가능성이 있을까요?

제프리 샷 박사: 중국이 중-단기적으로 CPTPP 요건을 통과할 가능성은 매우 낮다고 생각합니다. 그리고 중국도 이미 이를 인지하고 있으며, 정치적인 이유로 대만의 CPTPP 가입을 사실상 막고 있기 때문에 자신들이 여전히 혜택을 볼 수 있다는 점을 인식하고 기본적으로 그 가정에서 일하고 있다고 생각합니다.

유장희 박사: 감사합니다. 한 가지 더 질문하겠습니다. 우크라이나-러시아 전쟁이 언제 끝날지, 이스라엘과 하마스 전쟁은 언제 끝날지 많은 사람들이 궁금해하고 관심을 갖고 있습니다. 이 시점에서 많은 국제 경제학자와 국제 정치학자들은 소위 위

스퍼게이트에 대해 걱정하고 있습니다. 위스퍼게이트는 전쟁이 AI 전쟁과 같은 전자 전쟁으로 확대되고 있다는 것을 의미합니다. 현재 많은 드론과 기타 많은 전자 장비가 사용되고 있으며 이러한 종류의 전자 전쟁의 수위는 날로 높아지고 있습니다. 이것이 전쟁이 끝나지 않는 이유입니다. 러-우 전쟁 및 이스라엘-하마스 전쟁도 전자 역량을 과시하는 한 곧 끝나지 않을 듯 합니다. 어떻게 보시는지요?

제프리 샷 박사: 제가 오늘 강연을 시작할 때 이 부분을 언급한 이유 중 하나는 이것이 확대될 위험이 있다고 생각하기 때문입니다. 새로운 유형의 전쟁 방법론에 대한 박사님의 지적은 정확합니다. 이는 매우 심각한 문제라고 생각합니다. 우크라이나에서 그리고 중동에서 현재 이러한 심각성을 목격하고 있습니다.

저는 군사 전문가는 아니지만 이러한 공격이 계속됨에 따라 군사적 확전의 위험이 크다는 것을 알고 있습니다. 이스라엘은 그렇게 하겠다는 의지를 보였고, 그 결과 많은 무고한 민간인이 고통받거나 사망했습니다. 경제나 무역의 관점에서 볼 때 이스라엘의 대이란 보복으로 중동 전역에 적대감이 확대될 것이 우려됩니다. 또한 트럼프가 대통령이 되면 우크라이나가 러시아와 푸틴과의 나쁜 거래를 받아들이라는 압력이 더 커질 것이라는 점도 우려됩니다. 유럽인들이 훨씬 더 취약한 위치에 있다고 느낄 것이기 때문에 미국과 유럽의 관계는 악화될 것입니다.

하지만 여기에는 또 다른 측면이 있습니다. 저보다 더 잘 아실 겁니다. 우크라이나와 중동에 대해 이야기하면서 빼놓으셨지만 우크라이나 전쟁의 나쁜 부작용 중 하나는 러시아와 북한 간의 군사적 관계가 심화되었다는 것입니다. 러시아가 북한의 전쟁 물자 의존도가 높아지면서 북한 정권이 한반도에서 행동할 때 조금 더 기동성이나 유연성을 발휘할 수 있는 여지를 주었습니다. 그래서 상당히 걱정스럽습니다. 사실 저는 중국인들에게도 상당히 걱정해야 한다고 말했습니다. 왜냐하면 북한 주민들이 중국의 압력과 강압에서 벗어나 좀 더 독립성을 확보할 수 있기 때문입니다. 저도 이 부분에 대해 매우 걱정하고 있고 정치 지도자들이 이 부분에 집중하길 바랍니다. 한국에 매우 중요하고 중대한 문제이기 때문에 경계를 높일 필요가 있습니다.

유장희 박사: 맞습니다. 우리 한국 사람들은 러시아와 북한 관계의 새로운 발전에 대해 매우 걱정하고 있습니다. 그리고 북한이 러시아에 다소 공격적으로 접근하는 것 때문에 중국과 북한의 외교 관계에 어떤 종류의 변화를 느끼고 있습니다. 이는 최근 동북아시아의 지정학적 질서에서 우리가 발견한 새로운 차원 중 하나입니다.

전광우 이사장: 감사합니다. 오늘은 채팅창을 통해서도 많은 질문들이 들어오고 있습니다. 이 중 한 가지 질문을 읽어드리겠습니다.

통찰력 있는 발표를 해주셔서 정말 감사합니다. 한국의 CPTPP 가입 가능성에 대해 여러 번 강조하셨는데요, 트럼프의 압박으로부터 한국을 보호할 수 있을 것이라고도 말씀하셨습니다. CPTPP 가입을 통해 한국이 어떤 보호를 받을 수 있을지 좀 더 자세히 설명해 주시겠습니까? 또 기존 회원국들과 한국 정치권에서 보는 시각이 좀 다른 것 같습니다. 그런데 이번에는 일본의 새 총리가 친한파 정치인으로 여겨지고 한국 대통령이 일본과의 관계를 개선하려고 노력하고 있기 때문에 매우 기대가 큽니다. 어떻게 보시는지요? CPTPP 가입을 위해 어떻게 접근하는 것이 최선일까요?

제프리 샷 박사: 이 문제는 매우 중요한 문제이기 때문에 짧은 답변으로 그 중요성을 다 설명할 수는 없지만 몇 가지 요점을 말씀드리겠습니다. 우선 한국이 가입 신청을 결정하면 CPTPP에 참여할 수 있는 문이 활짝 열려 있을 것입니다. 다만, 한국이 CPTPP 요건을 충족하는 데 문제가 될 수 있는 몇 가지 분야가 있습니다. 기억하시겠지만, CPTPP는 크게 보면 환태평양경제동반자협정(TPP)이었습니다. 그리고 TPP는 한중일 FTA를 기초로 협상을 시작했습니다. 따라서 한국은 이미 요건 충족 측면에서 훨씬 앞서 있습니다. 그게 문제가 아니라고 생각합니다.

CPTPP의 특정 회원국들이 가입 대가로 한국에 추가적인 요구를 하지 않을까 하는 우려가 항상 있었습니다. 하지만 한국과 일본 등이 훨씬 더 긴밀하게 협력하면서 그런 우려는 많이 줄어들었다고 생각합니다. 기존 회원국들이 다음 달 위원회 회의에서 논의할 예정인 CPTPP의 실질적 범위 확대는 한국이 역내 이웃 국가들과 긴밀히 협력하여 보다 견고한 규칙을 만들고, 무역과 기후 문제 등을 해결하기 위해 디지털 무역을 촉진하고자 하는 많은 분야에서 추가적인 인센티브가 될 수 있을 것으로 생각됩니다.

따라서 한국이 가입할 수 있는 기회는 많습니다. 그리고 이를 위한 장애물은 매우 미미하다고 생각합니다. 트럼프 대통령이 백악관으로 복귀하면 한국에 대한 강압적인 노력이 차단될까요? 트럼프 대통령은 일대일 방식을 좋아합니다. 그리고 한국은 앞으로 한두 달 안에 12번째 회원국이 될 영국을 포함해 CPTPP의 긴밀한 파트너 및 동맹국들과 더욱 긴밀히 협력하고 있기 때문에 수적으로 어느 정도 안전장치를 마련할 수 있을 것으로 생각합니다.

최근 가입을 신청한 인도네시아처럼 다른 국가들도 가입 신청에 박차를 가할 것으로 보입니다. 이는 한국이 역내 다른 긴밀한 파트너, 무역 및 투자 파트너와 협력하는 데에도 매우 도움이 될 수 있습니다. 따라서 저는 한국이 CPTPP와 협력하고 그 관계를 활용해 미국과의 양자 관계를 공고히 하는 데 도움이 되는 훨씬 더 나은 위치에 놓일 수 있는 많은 가능성이 있다고 생각합니다.

전광우 이사장: 네, 감사합니다. 그럼 다른 질문을 하나 더 읽어드리겠습니다.

트럼프가 당선될 경우 한국에 미치는 영향, 특히 한미 FTA에 대해 한국의 이익을 방어할 수 없다는 지적은 매우 무섭게 들립니다. 트럼프가 말하는 이른바 '보편적 보호무역주의'가 한국과 같은 FTA 협정을 맺은 국가들에게도 무차별적으로 적용될 것이라고 생각하시나요? 과거에 트럼프 대통령이 사용했던 것처럼 협상 카드로 사용할 수 있을까요?

제프리 샷 박사: 물론 협상용 카드일 뿐이라는 주장도 있을 수 있습니다. 하지만 한국이 미국의 요구를 따르지 않으면 미국이 6개월 전에 통보하면 지소미아를 철회할 수 있다는 것은 실질적인 위협이 담긴 강압적인 협상 전술입니다. 그리고 트럼프는 첫 임기 때 거의 그렇게 할 뻔했습니다. 트럼프의 참모들이 트럼프 대통령이 앉아서 서명 하기 직전 대통령 책상에서 한미 FTA 탈퇴 결정 문서를 치워버렸다는 일화를 다들 기억하시죠? 저뿐만 아니라 많은 한국인 친구들의 등골을 오싹하게 만들었던 사건입니다. 우리가 매우 조심해야 할 부분이라고 생각합니다.

만약 그가 전반적으로 관세를 적용한다면, 예를 들어 10개의 관세를 전반적으로 적용한다면, 그것은 한미 FTA를 위반하는 것이고 우리의 모든 WTO 의무 등을 위반하는 것이고 심지어 미국 법률을 위반할 수도 있습니다. 이는 법원이 판단해야 할 문제입니다. 트럼프가 한발 물러서서 자동차에만 적용하겠다고 말할 수 있습니다. 자동차에 적용하면 한국의 대미 수출의 상당 부분이 해당되는 것입니다. 발생할 수 있는 피해의 정도는 다양하며, 반드시 전면적인 관세일 필요는 없지만 한미 FTA를 위반하고 한국 대미 수출업체를 차별하는 표적 관세일 수도 있습니다.

전광우 이사장: 네, 답변 감사합니다. 미국의 탄소 배출권 거래제, 즉 탄소 국경 조정과 유럽연합의 탄소 배출권 거래제 또는 면제가 조화를 이룰 수 있을까요?

제프리 샷 박사: 저는 탄소 정책 전반과 특히 국경 조정 메커니즘을 조정하거나 조화시키려는 미국과 유럽의 노력이 성공적

이지 못했다고 생각합니다. 철강과 관련하여 시도하는 데 집중해 왔지만 아무 진전이 없었습니다. 저는 이 문제는 매우 어렵다고 생각합니다. 만약 트럼프가 백악관으로 돌아온다면 관세 정책 조율에 관심이 없을 것 같습니다. 그는 일방적으로 행동하고 싶어 할 것입니다.

전광우 이사장: 감사합니다. 이번 질문은 거시경제에 관한 질문입니다.

트럼프 재선의 경우 달러화 약세와 금리인상 가능성이 있다고 말씀하셨는데요, 딜레마라고 할 수 있습니다. 트럼프 본인은 달러 약세를 좋아한다고 말했지만 동시에 다른 정책들은 인플레이션을 초래하여 금리를 더 높게 할 것이고, 일반적으로 금리가 높아지면 달러가 강해집니다. 그렇다면 트럼프가 추구하는 정책의 결과가 상충되는 경우, 트럼프는 어느 쪽을 더 선호할 것이라고 생각하십니까?

제프리 샷 박사: 문제를 아주 잘 설명해 주셨습니다. 트럼프가 원하는 것은 약달러를 통해 미국 수출을 늘리고 미국 내 제조업을 보호하는 것입니다. 그러나 말씀하신 것처럼, 그가 추진하는 모든 정책은 정반대의 결과를 초래할 것입니다. 그런데 아직 고려되지 않은 또 다른 요인이 있습니다. 트럼프는 연준 이사회에 대한 통제력을 강화하는 방안도 언급했는데, 그가 원하는 것은 달러 약세를 선호하고 따라서 인플레이션 압력에 직면하여 금리를 인상하지 않는 보다 순응적인 연준 이사회입니다. 이 경우 거시경제적 불균형이 시간이 지남에 따라 미국 경제에 거대한 불균

형과 왜곡을 초래할 수 있습니다. 트럼프 1기 때 그가 대법원 판사 세 명을 임명하는 데 성공해 다른 많은 영역에 변화를 가져온 것처럼, 연준 이사회를 대통령에 더 순응적이고, 더 투명하며, 금리에 대해 덜 강경하게 만들려고 할 수 있습니다.

전광우 이사장: 네, 답변 감사합니다. 방금 전 질문의 연장선상에서 한 가지 추가 질문을 드리겠습니다. 바이든 행정부 하에서 현재 강세를 보이고 있는 주식시장이 트럼프가 가지고 있는 모든 정책 수단을 고려할 때 그가 집권한 이후에도 이러한 강세를 이어갈 수 있을까요?

제프리 샷 박사: 저는 1960년대에 월스트리트에서 일했습니다. 높은 직책은 아니었지만 시장이 어디로 갈지 안다고 생각되면 돈을 베팅하고 다음 날 결과를 확인해야 한다는 것은 충분히 배웠습니다. 단기적으로 주식 시장 밸류에이션에 영향을 미칠 많은 요인이 있고, 이러한 거시경제적 효과 중 일부는 시간이 걸릴 것이라고 생각합니다. 따라서 주식 밸류에이션에 대해 생각하기는 매우 어렵지만 인플레이션으로 인한 영향은 분명히 있을 것이라고 생각합니다. 단기적으로나 중기적으로 인플레 압력이 급격히 증가할 것이며, 이는 미국의 생산과 생산 능력에 추가 비용을 부과하고 성장을 둔화시킬 것으로 예상됩니다. 그리고 이는 시간이 지남에 따라 주식 밸류에이션을 약화시킬 것입니다.

전광우 이사장: 답변 감사합니다. 오늘 박사님의 강연과 토론에 기초할 때, 이번 미국 대선에서 누가 승리하느냐와 관계 없이 미국의 대 중국 정책이 더욱 강경한 스탠스를 취할 것이라는 점

은 확실해 보입니다. 그리고 이는 중국 경제에 잠재적으로 치명적인 영향을 미칠 수 있다고 생각합니다.

잘 아시다시피 중국 경제는 각종 경기 부양책에도 불구하고 대규모 부채와 부동산 부문 채무 불이행, 인구 감소 및 구조적 문제로 침체에 직면해 있습니다. 이러한 가운데 미국의 추가 관세가 부과될 경우 중국의 경제 상황은 더욱 악화될 수 있습니다. 일각에서는 트럼프가 중국산 수입품에 60%의 관세를 부과할 경우 중국 성장률이 절반으로 줄어들어 GDP 성장률이 2%p 이상 감소할 것으로 예상하고 있습니다. 이는 중국 경제 뿐 아니라 아시아 지역, 북미까지도 파급 효과가 있을 수 있습니다. 이러한 경제적 도전을 고려할 때, 중국의 어려움이 해당 지역의 안보 환경을 불안정하게 만들 수 있다는 우려도 있는데요, 어떻게 보십니까? 우리가 직면한 이 엄청난 도전을 완화하기 위해 어떠한 조치가 필요할까요?

제프리 샷 박사: 아주 중요한 질문이고 앞으로 계속 논의해야 할 이슈라고 생각합니다. 오늘은 우선 몇 가지 요점을 말씀드리겠습니다. 중국 경제는 현재 10년 전이나 20년 전 만큼 역동적이지 않습니다. 과거보다는 더 성숙하고 더 발전해 있기 때문에 10% 성장률은 기대하기 어렵습니다. 지난 몇 년간의 다양한 충격으로 인한 시장의 금융 왜곡으로 인해 5% 성장 목표 마저도 도전에 직면해 있습니다.

하지만 중국은 거대한 내수 시장이 있습니다. 따라서 세계 최대 수출국이지만 재분배와 변화, 토착 기술 개발을 통해 수출 부진에 따른 충격을 내수를 바탕으로 상당 부분 극복할 수 있다고 봅니다. 시진핑 주석은 토착 기술 개발을 지원하고 보조금을 지급하는 데 매우 큰 베팅을 하고 있는 것 같습니다. 전기 자동차 시장을 보면 알 수 있습니다. 단기적으로 지방 정부 부채 문제 등으로 성장이 저조할 가능성이 높고, 추가적인 성장률 조정 가능성이 있지만, 감당할 수 있는 수준이라고 생각합니다.

트럼프가 대규모 관세를 부과하면 일부 생산에 변화가 있을 뿐만 아니라 상품이 생산되는 곳과 배송되는 곳에도 변화가 있을 것이라고 생각합니다. 단, 중국은 미국이 TPP에서 탈퇴했기 때문에 우선접근권을 갖고 있지 않은 아시아의 많은 중요한 국가들에 우선접근권을 가지고 있습니다. 미국은 일본과 FTA를 체결하지 않았으며, 많은 아세안 국가들과도 우선 협정을 맺지 않은 것과는 다른 상황입니다.

중국의 경제 상황이 너무 어려워서 관심을 돌리기 위해 정치적 또는 군사적으로 주의를 분산시키려고 할지는 모르지만, 안보 환경을 불안정하게 만드는 상황까지 초래되려면 중국의 경제와 정치 상황이 지금보다는 훨씬 더 나빠져야 한다고 생각합니다.

전광우 이사장: 네, 감사합니다. 트럼프와 해리스, 두 후보 중 누가 대통령이 되든 내년 미국 백악관 정세는 더욱 격변할 것으로 예상되는 만큼 우리도 잘 대응할 수 있도록 대비해야 할 것입니다. 제프리 샷 박사님, 다양한 주요 현안과 미국 새정부의 정책적 변화 가능성에 대해 훌륭한 강연과 토론을 해주셔서 대단히 감사드립니다. 함께해 주신 청중 여러분 감사합니다. 그럼 여기

서 마치겠습니다.

제프리 샷 박사: 감사합니다.

US Post-Election Trade Policy Outlook and Implications for China & Korea Economy

Jeffrey J. Schott

Jeffrey J. Schott

Mr. Schott is a senior fellow at the Peterson Institute of International Economics, working on international trade policy and economic sanctions. He has lectured at Princeton University and served as an adjunct professor at Georgetown University. He previously served as an official of the US Treasury Department in international trade and energy policy. He was also a member of the US State Department's Advisory Committee on International Economic Policy.

[Oct. 16, 2024]

US Post-Election Trade Policy Outlook and Implications for China & Korea Economy

Jeffrey J. Schott
Senior Fellow
Peterson Institute for International Economics (PIIE)

Jun Kwang-woo: Good morning, ladies and gentlemen, welcome to the IGE Webinar Forum.

Today, I am so very happy to have a distinguished guest speaker, Mr. Jeffrey Schott, one of the world's leading experts on international trade policy. He will be joining us live from Florida to discuss the very timely issues and new challenges for international trade at a time US Presidential election approaching in 3 weeks. Jeff will also talk about the implications of likely changing US trade policies in the new US Administration and their implications for Asia, especially China and Korea.

Mr. Schott is currently a Senior Fellow, working on international trade policy and economic sanctions at the Peterson Institute for International Economics(PIIE). He has taught at Princeton and Georgetown University, and has served as an official of the US Treasury Department in international trade and energy policy. Since 2003, Jeff has been a member of the US State Department's Advisory Committee on International Economic Policy. He holds a graduate degree with distinction from Johns Hopkins University.

Without further ado, let's welcome Mr. Jeffrey Schott who will speak for about 30 minutes first, followed by the Q&A until 10 am in Seoul time as scheduled.

Jeffrey J. Schott: Thank you very much, Chairman Jun. And good morning to everyone. It's always a great pleasure for me to join again with colleagues at the Institute for Global Economics(IGE).

It's a critical topic that we have on the agenda today, looking at the post-election trade policy outlook and It is a very difficult question to address because we are now three weeks to the day from the U.S. election. Votes are already being cast, early voting. And the race, according to all the polls, is a dead heat. And so we may not know right away who has won the race, whether it will be former President Trump or vice president Kamala Harris, but we do know that the election will make a big difference in the future course of U.S. economic policy. And this is something that I'm very concerned about.

For the past 50 years, I've worked on building the international economic order, working on writing the world trading rules on subsidies, helping the International Energy Agency(IEA) confront the oil cartel in the second oil shock, promoting economic integration in North America, and then across the Pacific with the KOR-US FTA and then the Trans-Pacific Partnership. and cautioning policymakers on the use and abuse of economic sanctions. We've made a lot of progress; Korea has made great strides, being one of the poorest economies in the world in the 1960s and now becoming an industrial superpower. That's the hard work and effort of many, many people.

But I fear that a lot of the progress that we have made in the post-war era is at risk of unraveling as cold trade wars and hot wars and new waves of protectionism masked by patriotic fervor threatened to disrupt or constrain international trade and investment. We've had an ongoing US-China cold trade war since 2018. Large US tariffs against Chinese imports into the United States and tit-for-tat trade retaliation by China against US goods and services and investment. And it looks like we are locked in a downward spiral of restriction and counter restriction in the US-China trade economic relationship.

At the same time, we have hot wars in the Ukraine and the Middle East in danger of spreading. We already I've seen threats to vital economic infrastructure, oil and gas pipelines and terminals in the region, disruptions of transport on the Black Sea and via the Suez Canal and the Red Sea as the

Houthis bomb shipping going through the Red Sea. This affects trade of many countries that have used the Suez Canal to shorten and improve trading networks between Europe and Asia.

We've seen growing use of national security exceptions and disregard for the WTO obligations. And these are undercutting support for the rules-based multilateral trading system. Negotiations in Geneva are ongoing. Work keeps going forward. but the results are very slim and sporadic. Efforts to advance work in the WTO on important issues like climate and on digital trade, seem to be getting nowhere. And that has led to efforts to look about reinforcing the trading system through bilateral and regional means. And that's something I'll talk about a little bit later.

The near-term outlook darkens depending on who is in the White House on January 20th, 2025. And so what I'd like to do is to spell out some of the challenges facing US policy and the different approaches that Mr. Trump and Vice President Harris would have in dealing with these issues.

Now, the economic agenda for United States in 2025. It focuses on a lot of things, many of them domestic, that don't resonate very widely on the international scene, but will have a big impact on U.S. domestic and international economic policy. First and foremost, I believe, would be the efforts to revise or extend the 2017 tax cuts that Donald Trump passed in the first year of his administration, and that are due to expire by the end, many of which are due to expire by the end of next year.

For Trump, he will want to extend and even deepen some of the tax cuts, thinking that those tax cuts will spur economic growth and pay for themselves, though it's very seldom that that has happened in the past and there's no evidence in the economics profession that that would happen again. Vice President Harris wants to pare back many of these tax cuts, particularly those benefiting the rich and upper middle class, to devote more revenues to social programs to deal with the underprivileged in U.S. society. That, of course, would take time. Additional effort and acts of Congress that may be hard to come by in 2025, because the Congress seems to be headed to be as divided between Democrats and Republicans as the presidential race looks to be in November. And it's unclear right now, whether which party will control the Senate, which party will control the House of Representatives, and which party and which candidate will win the White House. But in any event, there will be very slim majorities making that determination in the election in three weeks' time.

Now, there's also the task of rebuilding U.S. military and reinforcing industries vital to national security. Some of that is taking place as a result of the Inflation Reduction Act and focusing on rebuilding and upgrading the U.S. semiconductor industry. But there is also a need to upgrade U.S. military establishment and in addition, our not only manpower, but our equipment, particularly in ships. Given the nature of the hot and threatened hostilities in the Middle East and in Asia, US actually needs more ships. And we will need to have help from our allies if that's going to happen, but there's going to require a lot of spending. So more spending on tax cuts, more spending on military and industrial development.

Then also confronting Chinese competition at home and abroad via new tariffs. I think both candidates will move forward on that. And that will include non-tariff barriers affecting Chinese trade and foreign direct investment. And it will require coordination on US export controls, blunting technology transfer to Chinese firms and closer alignment of US, Korean and Japanese policies in particular. Next year will also mark a time when the U.S. will have to begin preparing for this mandated six-year review of the U.S.-Mexico-Canada agreement, where conflicts over autos and energy and agriculture and judicial reforms recently enacted in Mexico will threatened new controversies and conflicts between the three North American partners and could lead to great frictions in that integration arrangement. Indeed, threats from Donald Trump could even undercut the ability to use the power of the United States use Mexico as a base for nearshoring. So much for nearshoring if you are thinking of moving from East Asia to North America and finding investment opportunities for production to ship to the United States from Mexican facilities.

Finally, confronting Russian aggression via economic and military support will require economic and military support for Ukraine and will require tighter economic sanctions affecting global oil markets. And this is an area where the candidates will differ very, very broadly and could have very profound effects for the world economy and for world peace. Mr. Trump, frankly, seems willing to cut a good deal for Vladimir Putin to say, save U.S. money that would otherwise be spent on securing the Ukrainian economy and military. Vice President Harris would continue the support for Ukraine, but then be faced with a tough job, tough decision of whether to strengthen and broaden U.S. economic sanctions, which would have to hit oil markets much harder than they have so far.

Essentially, Mr. Putin has gotten a pass on real harm to the Russian economy because he has been able to continue to sell oil on world markets. And that has brought in several hundred billion dollars a year in revenues that has allowed him to turn the Russian economy into a war-focused economy with lots of distortions in it, but capable of continuing the War effort. Tightening those sanctions to limit the oil would have profound effects on global oil prices that would affect Mr. Putin, to be sure, but would also raise costs for consumers in Western countries and in East Asia. Now, what this all means, as the introduction to my book, deeper dive into trade policy, is that there will be key consequences on how the next US president responds to all of these situations.

Whatever happens, these priorities of action on the economic agenda will require additional federal revenues, and probably some cuts to some programs and benefits, including possibly the Inflation Reduction Act and the CHIPS and Science Act. The latter two are more likely under Donald Trump, who doesn't claim ownership of that and wants to ensure that the revenues in the budget are devoted to covering the tax cuts. Changes to U.S. tax policy policies, additional military expenditures, trade and investment interventions, and primary and secondary economic sanctions.

If you look at what will happen in markets as a result of this, it's clear that they will exacerbate the funding challenges of the US government and thus risk spiking inflationary pressures via burgeoning budget deficits and protection-induced price increases. If you put tariffs on a lot of goods, the price of those goods in the US market is going to go up for a lot of US consumers. And US consumers are both individual households and businesses that rely on imported components in their production processes. So Trump's plans, it is estimated, would add three to $4 trillion to the US budget deficit over a 10 year period. He dismisses this casually by saying that tariffs would raise lots of additional revenue. There is no evidence or there is no math that gets him that gets to that type of conclusion, except through the fantasy of the of the increasing tariff that is not going to result in a stronger U.S. economy, but will result in bigger budget deficits. Now, markets will recognize the obvious before politicians and interest rates will rise. And that will have an effect on dampening U.S. economic growth next year and have consequences that for the ability for the U.S. to trade and the amount that the U.S. will trade and invest and the attractiveness of the United States as an investment locale.

Now the implications for US trade policy in 2025. This is probably what everybody was thinking I'd start with, but I think we needed to get to the point to recognize that a lot of what is going to happen is going to be affected by this budget crunch. in the United States and whether or not U.S. trade policy contributes to improving or making it worse. And in most respects, I think trade policy will make it worse. Certainly, for either Trump or Harris, U.S. trade policy will be more inward looking than internationalist but much more inward looking for Trump than Vice President Harris, who has tried to maintain a more traditional international posture for the United States.

Domestic politics will increase pressure for migration controls. This has become a hot button political issue in the United States, particularly in the Southwest and among many of the sort of states, borderline states that will determine in part who wins the election in November. National security restrictions on steel and aluminum and other tech products will continue. So will the China trade war tariffs. That's going to be the same under Trump or Harris, though the implementation and the extension of the existing restrictions and interventions will differ between the two. And I'll get into that in a moment. Export controls against China, Russia, Iran, North Korea on sensitive technologies will broaden and deepen.

And I think that is happening and will happen regardless of whether it's Trump or Harris in the White House. Though the focus will be more on China and less on Russia if it's Mr. trump in the White House. Finally, anti-China trade and investment policies will be extended to constrain or decouple the two economies. And we've already seen this happening as President Biden has continued many of Trump's anti-China tariffs and restrictions. This has led to Chinese export expansion via third countries. And that in turn will provoke U.S. to pressure countries like Korea and Mexico, members of ASEAN, to limit their ties with China. But for many of these countries, China is a bigger trading partner than the United States. And that will put them between a rock and a hard place.

So, what's likely to happen on trade policy if Trump returns to the White House or if Harris is elected president?

Let me start with Trump. He says a lot of things off the top of his head. How much he will do or even want to do is an open question. But increasingly, tariffs seem to be at the core of his economic agenda and migration controls at the heart of his political agenda. And so that, among all the things he's planning to do, I think are much surer bets in the early days of a new Trump administration. I think he will quickly act on his campaign pledge to raise all U.S. tariffs by 10%. Plus, an additional 50 on Chinese goods using national security and emergency powers under Section 232 and the international emergency economic powers act.

Now, there is some legal controversy about whether those emergency powers can be deployed for across the board tariffs that really have a commercial justification. And so there could be challenges in court. And if so, in the short run, at least, the initial tariff increases could target China and national security sectors such as aluminum and steel, and autos. You might say, well, how is auto sector a national security issue? One could make the same point about steel and aluminum. And I'll get to the answer from a Trump point of view on that in a moment.

There's another bullet point that has been left to offer this slide that is critical and that is large uh trump would call for and enact with existing authorities uh available to the president a large deportation of migrants, perhaps on a scale as great, if not greater, than that occurred in the Eisenhower administration in the early 1950s, likely to affect more than 1 million workers. This forced deportation or a roundup and process of deportation would cause a large negative shock to the U.S. labor supply, leading to more inflation and less output. And you know what that means. That means stagflation. The result would be declines in GDP and a drop in durable manufacturing jobs, just the opposite of what Trump predicted. thinks would happen. This actually, this impact on the labor market, these shocks through the labor market of migration policies could be even greater than the initial tariff shock that comes from additional tariffs. So that is something that is really serious that needs to be looked at.

Tariffs on China will prompt retaliation against US exports and anti-circumvention via transshipment and sourcing from overseas Chinese factories in Southeast Asia and Latin America. This will lead to pressure, like Biden has already put on Mexico, to revisit policies on importation of goods and screening of investment from China in Mexico. But these countries benefit greatly from having Chinese production move from inland China to Vietnam or Malaysia or Mexico or elsewhere in Latin America. And so there will be some sharp problems with this type of policy if it begins to put in restrictions, not only trying to coerce our friendly trading partners from doing more business with China. But enforcing that coercion through restricting access of goods from friendly countries like Mexico and Malaysia and Vietnam and others into the U.S. market. This is a concern.

In the past, Trump has imposed duties against US friends and allies on steel and aluminum, and he could do so again to try to blunt China's efforts at circumventing the trade war tariffs. What about compliance with world trade rules? Well, that never stopped Trump before. And the U.S. neglect and we're likely to see U.S. neglect and violation of WTO obligations continue and possibly even the withdrawal from the WTO itself, like Trump did with the TPP in early 2017. trump's also likely to drop the indo-pacific economic framework initiative because it's a Biden initiative and he doesn't want to be associated with it.

But there's more that Trump would do. First is the focus on the U.S. trade deficit with Korea, especially in autos. This is something that economists learn in Econ 101 is not the way you go about doing international trade policy or economic relations. But this is something that Trump is always focused on. And the growing U.S. trade, merchandise trade deficit with Korea is a very attractive target for his attention. U.S. merchandise deficit is running this year at an annual rate of almost $60 billion. And the deficit in the auto sector with Korea is more than $43 billion on an annualized basis this year.

So focusing on the deficit with Korea and on how it is concentrated I think leads to the conclusion I reached in the previous slide that Trump could seek to impose new tariffs on automobiles to protect the economy. Sharply raised the MFN tariff of two and a half percent that allows most cars to come into the United States, whether they meet FTA or rules of origin or not. Now, Trump could threaten to disrupt the chorus FTA like he did with NAFTA, unless Korea changes policies to meet U.S. demands regarding defense burdens, regarding foreign direct investment in the U.S. in autos and semiconductors, regarding alignment with U.S. policies on export control. There are many areas of economic coercion that Trump is fond of using, in some ways quite similar to what Xi Jinping does in his neck of the woods.

Now, under Trump, climate policies would be downgraded. There could be a cutback in some of the IRA subsidies and other climate incentives not supported by big oil or the big three automakers, and those could be reduced or defunded. But there's one area where Trump could do something that seems to be pro-climate, but actually isn't rationalized in that way. He might support a U.S. carbon border adjustment mechanism measure, essentially new carbon tariffs, not for climate purposes, but to generate additional revenues from carbon intensive imports, hitting steel, hitting aluminum, hitting other products that have a big carbon footprint.

Note that I have not mentioned exchange rate policy. And this is also an important part of Trump's economic program that could affect international trade and investment. Trump wants to have a weak dollar. He thinks that will encourage U.S. exports and supplement U.S. tariffs to protect the U.S. market. But the policies that he is pushing essentially would raise interest rates because they would spike the budget deficit. Interest rates would go up and that would have at least a neoconflict or medium-term effect to drive up the value of the dollar, just the opposite of what he wants to do. This is a broader problem for the US economy if Trump comes into power, but it also has important ramifications for trade policy.

I can spend less time on the trade policy priorities under Kamala Harris if she is elected. Because she is starting from the base of the current administration's policies. But compared to, but she would moderate those policies in important ways. Compared to Trump, Harris would treat friends and allies more like friends and allies. And this could lead to even more stronger U.S.-Korea collaboration on semiconductors. I think this is very important.

She recognizes the importance of having a strong and dynamic high-tech industries and advanced research and development capabilities. And so this would be a priority sector to invest in for a Harris administration. She also would recognize the US's increased reliance on Korean shipbuilding to support both commercial transport and defense. And I think we would see a much broader alliance and linkage between the US and Korea ship defense establishment and relying more on Korea to help us rebuild our shipping capabilities. There'd be more coordination on, certainly more closely on economic security policies, sanctions and export controls.

And I haven't gone into too much about sanctions policy, but that could be another flashpoint relating to both the hostilities with Russia and China as the U.S. imposes stricter and more intrusive secondary sanctions affecting financial institutions that could have an impact or could have collateral damage on the trade and investment of Western countries with China and Russia. I think the big area of difference, obviously, between Harris and Trump is that, unlike Trump, there would be more focus on the climate trade nexus, including on plurilateral initiatives, and less overt threat to change the course FTA.

I think Kamala Harris has been a strong supporter. of climate initiatives. She voted against the US-Mexico-Canada agreement because it had a very weak environmental chapter that did not mention the words climate change. And so I think she would put much more focus on working on the nexus of trade and climate issues and trying to work more closely with countries that have been taking more steps than the United States has in recent years to develop effective programs for carbon mitigation and the advancement of renewable technologies. She would maintain China-specific trade restrictions and investment controls. I think she would continue the Indo-Pacific initiatives under Pillar 2, the supply chain resilience, and Pillar 3 with regard to climate, projects.

These are two areas where the United States and Korea have been working very closely together and where IPEF is actually providing additional areas for bilateral cooperation. But there's no sign that Kamala Harris would give more priority to revising or upgrading the WTO. And therefore, the current drift in the WTO might be continued, though I don't think she would go as far as trying to disrupt the organization, but she wouldn't. She wouldn't. advance it as much as it needs given the current situation in world markets.

So let me conclude with policy implications for Korea. I think Korea has to prepare for the extension and possible deepening of the US-China trade war with concomitant pressure to align with US export controls. So there will be pressure. I think it will be more coercive under Trump. It will be more cooperative as allies should be working together under President Harris. Don't expect the KOR-US FDA to protect and shield Korean interests from new protectionist measures, including higher auto tariffs, if Trump returns to power.

It didn't help with the 232 steel tariffs when he was president before, and it won't help if he's president again. The U.S. commitment, as I just said, to the multilateral trading system will be tepid at best under Harris, but negligible under Trump, who could withdraw from the WTO like he did from the TPP. And finally, and this probably deserves a meeting all of its own to focus on this last point, to reinforce the rules-based trading system, Korea should work more closely with other mid-sized powers to upgrade and expand trade rules bilaterally, regionally, and in the WTO in an effort to spur more trade and investment and promote economic growth.

One important way to do so would be to participate in the

CPTPP. That group is now undertaking a review of the first five years operations of the agreement, and it is planning to expand its membership. and to extend its substantive coverage, making it a much more attractive integration arrangement for Korea to join. I've argued that Korea should have joined when the agreement was initially pulled together, but I think it's never too late to take advantage of a good thing.

And if Trump wins the election, then Korea should apply to join the CPTPP right away, because that will be a big defense against some of the abuses that I think will be coming across the Pacific in a Trump administration. So I'm sorry to end on such a low note, but I hope I put enough on the table for our question period. Thank you very much.

Jun Kwang-woo: Thank you very much, Jeff, for your excellent presentation. And today we have invited one commentator, Dr. Yoo Jang-hee, whom you must know very well, who is one of the most distinguished and respected economic scholars in Korea on trade related issues. Dr. Yoo has previously served as President of the Korea Institute for International Economic Policy, Vice Chairman of the National Economic Advisory Committee and Chairman of the Commission on Shared Growth, among many other prominent positions. He is professor emeritus at Ewha Women's University. Now let me invite Dr. Yoo.

Yoo Jang-hee: Good morning, Chairman Jun. Thank you

very much for inviting me to this very important forum. And Hi, Jeff. It's really good to see you again. l I really appreciate your eloquent speech. I learned that the trade policy of the United States is going to be more and more complicated, particularly in dealing with the Korea's position as Trump is elected. I really appreciate that.

And I'd like to shift the gear a little bit to some of the points that you haven't covered this morning. That's about the APEC summit meeting. The APEC summit meeting is going to be held in Peru this year and in Korea, Gyeongju in particular, Gyeongju city next year. Since both US and China are the major members of the APEC, I'm sure the U.S. leader and the Chinese leader will get together in Peru this year in November, right after the U.S. presidential election.

And also they're going to get together in Gyeongju next year. As that happens, I'm sure these two leaders will be able to have good chances to talk to each other and then try to understand each other better, particularly in dealing with the trade policies. What kind of expectations do we have as far as this APEC summit meeting is concerned this year and next year?

Jeffrey J. Schott: Well, that's a very good point because one of the problems we face with the trade wars and the trade tensions globally is a lack of trust. And unless you have person to person, you know, meetings and relationships, it is very hard to overcome the mistrust that builds up in domestic politics. So I've always thought very important that we maintain channels of communication, even when we were going through and are going through difficult periods. But we don't want the other side to misinterpret, misunderstand, and misjudge what the other side is doing.

So for that reason alone, the apex situation summit meetings will be invaluable. I think there are areas where there is room for the United States and China to work more closely together. and to benefit particularly with the support of other APEC countries. And in the area of climate change, that could be the one area where we have common purpose, where Korea and Japan and others could contribute to a more balanced discussion and perhaps new initiatives. And where the world, there is no effective result unless the United States and China are participating in a climate carbon mitigation agreement. I hope progress can be made there in APEC.

Could it happen in CPTPP? I think one of the areas where the CPTPP members are thinking of expanding their substantive coverage is in the area of dealing with trade and climate. And if they could invite member countries, countries seeking accession to the agreement and other important outsiders like the United States and the European Union, you might have the foundations for a plurilateral agreement that could be done in the CPTPP context too.

Yoo Jang-hee: Would there be any possibilities that China would be invited to CPTPP in any case?

Jeffrey J. Schott: I think the prospects for China passing the CPTPP requirements in the near to medium term are very low. And I think the Chinese have already recognized that and are basically working off of that assumption, recognizing that they still benefit by their application because they're effectively, for political reasons, blocking the accession of Chinese Taipei into the CPTPP.

Yoo Jang-hee: Thank you, Jeff. May I add one more question? You see a lot of people are asking and interested in knowing when the Ukraine-Russia war will end and when Israel and Hamas war will end. At this point of time, many international economists and international political scientists are worried about the so-called Whisper gate. Whisper gate being that the war is escalating towards electronic wars, like AI wars. There are many drones and many other electronic equipment are being used at the moment and then the degree of this sort of electronic wars is going up every day. That's the reason why the war is not going to end. Wars in Ukraine and in Israel will not end soon as long as they are, showing off their electronic capacities. So would you take this like a different kinds of war in mind?

Jeffrey J. Schott: Well, one of the reasons why I mentioned that right at the beginning of my talk today, that I think this risks escalation. I think the point you made about the new types of warfare methodologies is exactly right and very troublesome. But We're seeing that in Ukraine, we're seeing that in the Middle East.

I'm not a military expert, but I know that there is a big risk of escalation, military escalation, as these attacks continue. The Israelis have shown a willingness to do that, and many innocent civilians have suffered or died as a result. But from an economic or trade point of view, I am concerned that there will be an expansion of hostilities across the Middle East with Israeli retaliation against Iran. And I'm also concerned that if Trump becomes president, there will be more pressure on Ukraine to accept a bad deal with Putin, with Russia. And that will exacerbate U.S.-European relations because the Europeans will feel they're in a much more vulnerable position.

But there is another aspect to this. that you know more about than I do. and you left it out in talking about Ukraine and the Middle East. that is one of the bad side effects of the Ukraine war has been a deepening of the military relationship between Russia and North Korea as Russia becomes more reliant on war material from North Korea. It gives the North Korean regime a little more room for maneuver or flexibility in its actions on the Korean peninsula. And that worries me quite a bit. And in fact, I told the Chinese it should worry the Chinese quite a bit. And because it gives the North Koreans a bit more independence away from Chinese pressure and coercion. So this is something I'm also very worried about and would hope that political leaders would focus on. But I would value your expertise because it's such an important and critical issue for South Korea.

Yoo Jang-hee: You're right. We South Koreans are very much worried about that kind of new development in the relationship between Russia and North Korea. And then we feel some kind of change in the diplomatic relationship between China and North Korea because of the North Korea's like, you know, approaching Russia rather aggressively. So that is one of the new dimensions that we have recently found in the geopolitical order of Northeast Asia.

Jun Kwang-woo: Thank you very much, Dr. Yoo, for sharing your thoughts with us this morning. Thank you, Jeff. And we are getting quite a few questions through our chat room so let me pass on one question. Let me read it for you, Jeff:

Thank you very much for your insightful presentation. Regarding your comments on Korea's potential accession to the CPTPP, could you elaborate on how joining the CPTPP would provide Korea with this protection? So a little bit of elaboration, and you can also touch on how best we can somehow access this, because apparently there are some different views about the existing members and Korea itself and political circles and how smooth the process of joining the CTPP is not, it could also be questionable. But I have high expectations this time because a new Prime Minister of Japan is seen as a pro-Korea politician while the President of Korea is trying to improve our relationship, bilateral relationship with Japan.

Jeffrey J. Schott: Well, this is a critical issue and I can't give it the importance it deserves in a short answer but let me make a couple of points. First of all, the door should be wide open for Korean participation in CPTPP once Korean officials decide to apply for membership. There are a few areas where there would be problems for Korea meeting the CPTPP requirements. If you recall, the CPTPP was largely the TPP. And the TPP started negotiations based on the foundation of the chorus FTA. So Korea is already way ahead of the game in terms of meeting the requirements. That I don't think is the issue.

There was always the concern about whether certain members of the CPTPP would make additional demands on Korea as a price of entry. But I think that has gone down quite a bit as Korea and Japan and others have been working much more closely together. the expansion of the substantive coverage of the CPTPP, which the existing members are planning to discuss at their commission meeting next month, I think also would provide an additional incentive because this would be in many areas where Korea wants to work closely with its neighbors in the region to build more solid rules, to promote digital trade to work on trade and climate issues and the like.

So there's a lot of upside for Korea to join. And I think very, very minimal obstacles for that. Would it block coercive efforts if President Trump is back in the White House against Korea? President Trump likes to operate on a one-on-one basis. And Korea working more closely with its close partners and allies in the CPTPP, which now will include the United Kingdom, which will become the 12th member of the CPTPP in the next month or two, I think will provide some safety in numbers.

And other countries are likely to try to accelerate their membership applications, such as Indonesia, which just applied. And this could also be very helpful for Korea working with other close partners, trade and investment partners in the region. So I think there's a lot of possibilities that would put Korea in a much better position working with the CPTPP and using that relationship to help support its bilateral relations with the United States.

Jun Kwang-woo: Okay, thank you very much. Let me read another question for you, Jeff:

Your point about the implications for Korea, especially the KORUS FTA, of not being able to defend Korea's interests if Trump is elected sounds very scary to me. Do you think that Mr Trump's so-called universal terraformation will be applied indiscriminately to countries with FTAs like Korea?

Will it, uh, will it, uh, will it just be used as a bargaining chip, uh, as Mr Trump has used it in the past?

Jeffrey J. Schott: It certainly is going to be argued that it's just a negotiation card. But it is a coercive negotiating tactic with the real threat that the United States could withdraw on six months' notice from the course FTA if Korea didn't abide by US demands. And Trump almost did that before. in his first term. Recall the insider book that noted how Trump's chief of staff removed the decision memo to withdraw from FTA from the president's desk before he had the chance to sit down and sign it. That, I think, sent chills through my spine, and that of many, many, many Korean friends. So I think that's a something that we have to be very cautious about.

Now, if he applied across the board tariffs, let's say the 10 across the board tariffs, that would violate the chorus FDA and it would violate all our WTO obligations and the like, and it may even violate US law. That's something the courts would have to determine. But he may back down and say, oh, I'm going to not apply it to our free trade partners, but I'm going to apply it to automobiles. And this is the point I made in my presentation. Applying it to automobiles would cover a good proportion of Korean exports to the United States. So there are degrees of harm that could arise and it doesn't have to be necessarily just the across the board tariff, but it could be targeted tariffs that violate the chorus FTA and discriminate against the Korean exporters to the United States.

Jun Kwang-woo: Okay, Thank you for the discussion. I still have several questions from our audiences.

Is there be any harmonization of US CBAM, that's carbon border adjustment, and EU CBAM or exemption going on?

Jeffrey J. Schott: I believe US European efforts to try to coordinate or harmonize carbon policies in general and border adjustment mechanisms in particular have not been successful. And indeed, they have focused on trying to do it with regard to steel. And those talks have gotten nowhere. And so I think that's it's very difficult. And if Trump returns to the White House, I don't think there'd be any interest in coordinating tariff policies. He'd want to act unilaterally.

Jun Kwang-woo: Thank you. This question is rather macroeconomic one rather than a trade question.

You said that there is a possibility of a weaker dollar and interest rate hikes in the event of Trump's re-election, which can be described as a dilemma. Trump himself has said that he likes a weak dollar, but at the same time, other policies will lead to inflation, which will cause interest rates to rise, and generally, when interest rates rise, the dollar strengthens. So, if the results of the policies Trump is pursuing are conflicting, which do you think Trump will prefer?

Jeffrey J. Schott: Exactly. You put it very, very well. And what Trump wants is a weak dollar to boost US exports and protect US manufacturing at home. But as you said, all the policies he's pursuing would lead to exactly the opposite result, but there's another factor that hasn't come into play. He's also talked about having more control over appointments to the Federal Reserve Board, and what he wants is a more compliant Federal Reserve Board that favors a weaker dollar and therefore doesn't raise interest rates in the face of inflationary pressures.

So if he gets to that point, some of the concerns that we have about trade policy would seem rather small compared to the huge imbalances and distortions in the US economy that would result over time because of these macroeconomic imbalances. So the question is a very pertinent one, but it is not just about economics, it is about politics. And this is an area where Trump, who has been so successful in appointing three members of the Supreme Court, which has led to changes in other areas, now wants to reshape the Federal Reserve Board to make it more compliant to the president and more transparent and less hawkish on interest rates.

Jun Kwang-woo: Okay, fine. One further question related as an extension of the question before, given all the policy tools Mr. Trump has on his plate, would the current bullish stock market under Biden administration be able to continue in the coming years as he comes on board?

Jeffrey J. Schott: I worked on Wall Street in the 1960s. I was not in a very high position, but I learned enough to know that if you think you know where the market is going, put your money on the table and see if you have any money the next day. I think there are a lot of factors that will come into play short term that will change affect stock market valuations and some of these macroeconomic effects will take some time to play through. So it would be very difficult to think about stock valuations, but clearly there will be some impact as inflation. Spikes in the near to medium term. And that will impose additional costs on production, productive capacity in the United States and dampen growth. And that has to lead over time to. Weaker stock valuations.

Jun Kwang-woo: Thank you for your response. Regardless of the election outcome, one thing seems clear. U.S. policy will likely remain tough on China. From my perspective, and that of many experts, the potential impact on China's economy could possibly be devastating. Despite recent stimulus efforts, China's economy is in a downturn, facing low growth, large debt, real estate defaults, demographic challenges, and structural issues.

On top of this, additional tariffs, particularly if Trump's proposed 60% tariff on Chinese imports is implemented, could halve China's growth, resulting in a loss of over two percentage points of GDP. This would have a significant impact on China's economy, potentially causing spillover effects, particularly in East Asia and North America.

Given these economic challenges, I'm concerned that China's struggles could destabilize the security environment in the region. If this is a reasonable expectation, what steps do you think should be taken to mitigate these challenges, particularly in our part of the world?

Jeffrey J. Schott: That is a big, big question, incredibly important question, one that can't be answered sufficiently before the workday is over.

But let me make a couple of points. And certainly, this is an issue we're going to have to continue to discuss as we continue to meet. The Chinese economy is not as dynamic as it was a decade or two ago. It's more mature, it's more developed. And so 10 growth rates are not on the horizon. 5 growth rates are facing a challenge because of the financial distortions in the market caused by the various shocks of the past couple of years. But China, is a huge domestic market.

So even though it's the world's biggest exporter, it can still get by to a significant extent by redistribution and changes and indigenous technological development. And it seems to me that Xi Jinping is placing a very big bet on supporting and subsidizing indigenous technological development. to find the breakthroughs that will lead to world-class production advancing as is occurring in the electric vehicle market. at least at the low end of that market.

So I've heard a variety of opinions on this from Chinese economists. I was in Shanghai last month, had Chinese visitors in Washington, and I'm sure we'll hear a lot more about it next week during the annual meetings of the World Bank. and the International Monetary Fund in Washington. Excuse me. But I think there is a good chance that Chinese growth will underperform, which will, in most respects in the short run, just mean additional adjustment challenges for the Chinese government dealing with municipal and provincial authorities. I think that's manageable in the short term.

I don't think if Trump put on these massive tariffs, there would be a shifting in some production, but also a shifting in where goods are produced and where they're shipped to. And remember, China has preferential access to a lot of important markets in the Asia Pacific region that the United States does not have because we pulled out of TPP, because we don't have a FTA with Japan, because many ASEAN countries are not in a preferential agreement with the United States. So I'm not sure we're sort of pull these diverse strands together.

I'm not sure the situation would be so difficult in China economically that they would seek a more political or military distraction to try to divert attention. We saw evidence with the naval maneuvers around Taiwan in the past week. But I think destabilizing the security environment, I think things would have to be a lot worse in terms of the economics and the politics in China for that to happen.

Jun Kwang-woo: Thank you very much indeed. As we approach a more turbulent environment with the upcoming election, whoever wins the White House next year, we must be well-prepared. I appreciate your insightful advice and excellent analysis of the current situation, as well as what we can expect in the months and years ahead. Thank you again, Jeff.

Jeffrey J. Schott: Thanks a lot.

세계경제연구원 특별강연 간행물 목록

IGE Publications

Occasional Paper Series

1993

	Title	Author
93-01	Clintonomics and the New World Order: Implications for Korea-US Relations	C. Fred Bergsten
93-02	The Uruguay Round, NAFTA and US-Korea Economic Relations	Jeffrey Schott

1994

	Title	Author
94-01	Korea in the World: Today and Tomorrow	Paul Kennedy
94-02	US-Japan Technological Competition and Implications for Korea	Ronald A. Morse
94-03	The Problems of the Japanese Economy and their Implications for Korea	Toyoo Gyohten
94-04	Changing US and World Economies and their Market Prospects	Allen Sinai
94-05	Prospects for New World Monetary System and Implications for Korea	John Williamson
94-06	The Promises of the WTO for the Trading Community	Arthur Dunkel

1995

	Title	Author
95-01	Mexican Peso Crisis and its Implications for the Global Financial Market	Charles H. Dallara
95-02	The World Economic Trend and US Economic Outlook	Allen Sinai
95-03	New Games, New Rules, and New Strategies	Lester Thurow
95-04	The United States and North Korea Future Prospects	Robert Scalapino
95-05	US Foreign Policy toward East Asia and the Korean Peninsula	James A. Baker III
95-06	US Trade Tension with Japan and their Implications for Korea	Anne O. Krueger
95-07	Prospects for Northeast Asian Economic Development: Japan's Perspective	Hisao Kanamori

1996

	Title	Author
96-01	Trends of International Financial Market and Prospects of Global Economy in 1996	Allen Sinai
96-02	Future European Model: Economic Internationalization and Cultural Decentralization	Jørgen Ørstrøm Møller
96-03	Evolving Role of the OECD in the Global Economy	Donald Johnston
96-04	The Political Context and Consequences of East Asian Economic Growth	Francis Fukuyama
96-05	Korea's New Global Responsibilities	A. W. Clausen

1997

	Title	Author
97-01	East Asia in Overdrive: Multinationals and East Asian Integration	Wendy Dobson
97-02	American Security Policy in the Asia Pacific - Three Crisis and How We Dealt with Them	William Perry
97-03	Public Sector Reform in New Zealand and its Relevance to Korea	Donald Hunn

1998

	Title	Author
98-01	Global Cooperations and National Government: Why We Need Multilateral Agreement on Investment	Edward Graham
98-02	Korean-American Relations: The Search for Stability at a Time of Change	W. Anthony Lake
98-03	Korea: From Vortex to Hub of Northeast Asia	Donald P. Gregg
98-04	German Unification: Economic Consequences and Policy Lessons	Juergen B. Donges
98-05	Globalization and versus Tribalization: The Dilemma at the End of the 20th Century	Guy Sorman

1999

	Title	Author
99-01	Economic and Political Situation in North Korea and Security in Northeast Asia	Marcus Noland
99-02	The International Financial Market and the US Dollar/Yen Exchange Rate: An Overview and Prospects for the Future	Kenneth S. Courtis

	Title	Author
99-03	Prospects and Policy Recommendations for the Korean Economy and Other Asian Economies	Donald Johnston/ Hubert Neiss
99-04	Reflections on Contrasting Present-day US and Japanese Economic Performances	Hugh Patrick
99-05	Challenge for the World Economy: Where Do the Risks Lie?	Rudiger Dornbusch

2000

	Title	Author
00-01	North Korea-US Relationship: Its Current Condition and Future Prospects	Stephen W. Bosworth
00-02	Global New Economy: Challenges and Opportunities for Korea	Soogil Young
00-03	Global Trend in Financial Supervision	YongKeun Lee
00-04	Asia Grows, Japan Slows: Prospects for the World Economy and Markets	Kenneth S. Courtis
00-05	The Future of International Financial System and its Implications for Korea	Morris Goldstein
00-06	Prospects for Millennium Round Trade Negotiations and Korea-US Free Trade Agreement	Jeffrey Schott/ InBeom Choi
00-07	Prospects for the Multilateral Economic Institutions	Anne O. Krueger
00-08	Avoiding Apocalypse: The Future of the Two Koreas	Marcus Noland
00-09	Attracting FDI in the Knowledge Era	Andrew Fraser
00-10	The Economic and Foreign Policies of the New US Administration and Congress	C. Fred Bergsten
00-11	Korea and the US: Partners in Prosperity and Security	Stephen W. Bosworth
00-12	The Outlook for Asia and Other Emerging Markets in 2000	Charles H. Dallara/ Robert Hormats
00-13	Relationship between Corporation and Finance: Current Status and Prospects	Youngkeun Lee
00-14	How Should Korea Cope with Financial Globalization	James P. Rooney

2001

	Title	Author
01-01	The US Economy on the Brink? Japan on the Edge? Implications for Korea	Kenneth S. Courtis
01-02	The Economic Policy of the Bush Administration toward Korea	Marcus Noland

	Title	Author
01-03	Overcoming 3Cs	Jeffrey D. Jones
01-04	High Tech, The Consequences for our Relationship with Technology on our Lives and Businesses	John Naisbitt
01-05	Korea and the IMF	Stanley Fischer
01-06	The Status of Korea's Restructuring: An Outlook over the Next 10 Years	Dominic Barton
01-07	The World Dollar Standard and the East Asian Exchange Rate Dilemma	Ronald McKinnon
01-08	Europe's Role in Global Governance and Challenges to East Asia	Pierre Jacquet

2002

	Title	Author
02-01	Managing Capital Inflows: The Chilean Experience	Carlos Massad
02-02	Globalization and Korea: Opportunities and Backlash and Challenges	Martin Wolf
02-03	The US-Japan Economic Relationship and Implications for Korea	Marcus Noland
02-04	US Global Recovery: For Real? - Prospects and Risks	Allen Sinai
02-05	Globalization: A Force for Good	Patricia Hewitt
02-06	The World after 9/11: A Clash of Civilization?	Francis Fukuyama
02-07	Hanging Together: On Monetary and Financial Cooperation in Asia	Barry Eichengreen
02-08	The Global Economy Rebounds - But How Fast and For How Long? Issues and Implications for Korea and Asia	Kenneth S. Courtis
02-09	The US Economy and the Future of the Dollar: An Outlook for the World Economy	Marcus Noland
02-10	The Doha Round: Objectives, Problems and Prospects	Jagdish Bhagwati
02-11	The Outlook for Korea and the Global Economy 2002-2003	Paul F. Gruenwald
02-12	The US and World Economy: Current Status and Prospects	John B. Taylor
02-13	9/11 and the US Approach to the Korean Peninsula	Thomas C. Hubbard
02-14	The Outlook for US Economy, the Dollar and US Trade Policy	C. Fred Bergsten
02-15	New Challenges and Opportunities for the Global Telecommunications and Information Industries	Peter F. Cowhey

2003

	Title	Author
03-01	The US and World Economy: After the Iraq War	Allen Sinai
03-02	Korea in the OECD Family	Donald Johnston
03-03	The New Role of the US in the Asia-Pacific	Charles Morrison
03-04	The Global Economic Outlook and the Impact of President Bush's Economic Stimulus Package	Phil Gramm
03-05	Europe and Germany in Transition, Where Will the Economies Go?	Hans Tietmeyer
03-06	Regional Financial Cooperation in East Asia	Eisuke Sakakibara
03-07	The Global Exchange Rate Regime and Implications for East Asian Currencies	John Williamson

2004

	Title	Author
04-01	General Outlook on the US and World Economy in 2004	Allen Sinai
04-02	Korea after Kim Jong-il	Marcus Noland
04-03	US-Japan Relations and Implications for Korea	Hugh Patrick/ Gerald Curtis
04-04	China's Economic Rise and New Regional Growth Paradigm	Zhang Yunling
04-05	The Case for a Common Currency in Asia	Robert Mundell
04-06	A Foreign Businessman's Observations on Korean Economy and Other Things	William C. Oberlin

2005

	Title	Author
05-01	US Trade Policy after the 2004 US Election	Peter F. Cowhey
05-02	Asia in Transition and Implications for Korea	Dominic Barton
05-03	Post-Election US and Global Economies: Market Prospects, Risks, and Issues	Allen Sinai
05-04	The Korean Economy: A Critical Assessment from the Japanese Perspective	Yukiko Fukagawa
05-05	The Blind Man and the Elephant: Competing Perspectives on Global Imbalances	Barry Eichengreen
05-06	Mutual Interdependence: Asia and the World Economy	Anne O. Krueger

	Title	Author
05-07	The Impact of China and India on the Global Economy	Wendy Dobson
05-08	Economic Integration between East Asia and Asia-Pacific	Robert Scollay
05-09	Moody's Perspective on Korea's Ratings	Thomas Byrne

2006

	Title	Author
06-01	Oil Prices, Ben Bernanke, Inflation, and the Fourth Energy Recession	Philip K. Verleger
06-02	US and Global Economy and Financial Market Prospects: Picking up Steam	Allen Sinai
06-03	Korea-US FTA: A Path to Sustainable Growth	Alexander Vershbow
06-04	Japan's Foreign Policy for Economy and Japan-Korea FTA	Oshima Shotaro
06-05	Japan's Economic Recovery: Implications for Korea	Yukiko Fukagawa
06-06	M&A in the 21st Century and its Implications	Robert F. Bruner
06-07	Korea's Growing Stature in the Global Economy	Charles H. Dallara
06-08	Asian Economic Integration and Common Asian Currency	Eisuke Sakakibara
06-09	Measuring American Power in Today's Complex World and China "Rising": What Lessons for Today from the Past?	Paul Kennedy/ Bernard Gordon
06-10	- Whither China? - The Global Scramble for IT Leadership: Winners and Losers	- Richard N. Cooper - George Scalise

2007

	Title	Author
07-01	Korea and the United States - Forging a Partnership for the Future: A View from Washington	Edwin J. Feulner
07-02	Germany: Understanding for the Underperformance since Reunification	Juergen B. Donges
07-03	Seismic Shifts, the World Economy, and Financial Markets in 2007	Allen Sinai
07-04	Changing Economic Environment: Their Implications for Korea	Angel Gurría
07-05	The Feasibility of Establishing an East Asian FTA: A Chinese Perspective	Zhang Yunling
07-06	The Global Oil and Gas Market: Paradigm Shift and Implications for Korea	Fereidun Fesharaki

	Title	Author
07-07	The Changing World Economy and Implications for Korea	Anne O. Krueger
07-08	The Longest Recovery of the Japanese Economy: Prospects and Challenges	Yukiko Fukagawa
07-09	Digital Networked Economy and Global Corporate Strategy	Ben Verwaayen
07-10	Moving Forward on the KORUS FTA: Now for the Hard Time	Jeffrey Schott
07-11	The Korean Economy and the FTA with the United States	Barry Eichengreen
07-12	- The Outlook for East Asian Economic Integration: Coping with American Protectionism, Chinese Power, and Japanese Recovery - Economic Outlook for Korea and the Region	- David Hale - Jerald Schiff
07-13	- Why the US Will Continue to Lead the 21st Century? - The Outlook of the Indian Economy from Business Perspective: Implications for Korean Business	- Guy Sorman - Tarun Das

2008

	Title	Author
08-01	Successes of Globalization: the Case of Korea	Anne O. Krueger
08-02	The US "Risk" to Asia and Global Expansion	Allen Sinai
08-03	Europe's Slow Growth: A Warning for Korea	Guy Sorman
08-04	Global Challenges that Will Confront the Next US President	James A. Baker III
08-05	Current Status and Prospects of the Japanese Capital Markets	Atsushi Saito
08-06	Economic and Political Outlook for America and their Implications to the World	Phil Gramm
08-07	The Outlook of the Regional and Global Economic and Financial Situation: Perspectives on International Banking	Charles H. Dallara
08-08	Can South Korea Still Compete?	Guy Sorman
08-09	- Sovereign Wealth Funds: Perceptions and Realities - Global Financial Markets under Stress	- Robert C. Pozen - Jeffrey R. Shafer

2009

	Title	Author
09-01	Global and Regional Economic Developments and Prospects, and the Implications for Korea	Subir Lall
09-02	Competing in an Era of Turbulence and Transition	Deborah Wince-Smith
09-03	US and Global Economic and Financial Crisis: Prospects, Policies, and Perspectives	Allen Sinai
09-04	US Trade Policy in the Obama Era	Jeffrey Schott
09-05	Beyond Keynesianism	Justin Yifu Lin
09-06	- Current Crisis and the Impact on Developing Countries - Lessons from the Current Economic Crisis	- Danny Leipziger - Anne O. Krueger
09-07	- Obama, Can It Work? - The US-Korea Economic Partnership: Working Together in a Time of Global Crisis	- Guy Sorman - Jeffrey Schott

2010

	Title	Author
10-01	The EU in Transition in the New Global Paradigm: Opportunities for Korea	Jean-Pierre Lehmann
10-02	Aftermath of the 'Crises': US and Global Prospects, Legacies, and Policies	Allen Sinai
10-03	The Global Economy: Where Do We Stand?	Anne O. Krueger
10-04	- Japan and Korea in Globalization and its Backlash: Challenges and Prospects - An Overview of China: Economic Prospects and Challenges	- Yukiko Fukagawa - Danny Leipziger
10-05	- Emerging Markets and New Frontiers - Asia in the Global Economy	- Mark Mobius - Dominique Strauss-Kahn
10-06	Rebalancing the World Economy	Paul A. Volcker

2011

	Title	Author
11-01	After the Crisis: What Next in 2011 and 2012?	Allen Sinai
11-02	Safety and Economics of Nuclear Power	SoonHeung Chang
11-03	A Special Lecture on the Rebalancing of the Chinese Economy	Yu Yongding

	Title	Author
11-04	Reshaping the Global Financial Landscape: An Asian Perspective	Institute for Global Economics
11-05	- Economic Outlook and Future Challenges in Developing Asia - Europe's Financial Woes	- Haruhiko Kuroda - Richard N. Cooper
11-06	- Can the G20 Save Globalization and Multilateralism? - Markets, Economic Changes, and Political Stability in North Korea	- Danny Leipziger - Marcus Noland

2012

	Title	Author
12-01	US and Global Economy and Financial Markets in Turmoil: What Lies Ahead?	Allen Sinai
12-02	- Advancement and Education of Science and Technology University and Economic Growth - Prospects of the Eurozone Crisis and its Implications for the Global Economy	- Nam Pyo Suh - Hans Martens
12-03	- The US Elections in 2012 and the Future of US Asia-Pacific Policy - Current Economic Affairs and the Financial Market - An Optimist View on the Global Economy	- Charles Morrison - Charles H. Dallara - Guy Sorman
12-04	- FTAs, Asia-Pacific Integration and Korea - The Eurozone Crisis: Update and Outlook	- Peter A. Petri - Nicolas Véron
12-05	- China's New Leadership and Economic Policy Challenges - Can the WTO Be Resuscitated? Implications for Korea and the Asia Pacific	- Andrew Sheng - Jean-Pierre Lehmann

2013

	Title	Author
13-01	After the Crisis: What Next in 2011 and 2012?	Allen Sinai
13-02	The Eurozone Crisis and its Impact on the Global Economy	Guntram B. Wolff
13-03	- The European Sovereign Debt Crisis: Challenges and How to Solve Them - The Global Outlook: Grounds for Optimism, but Risks Remain Relevant	- Andreas Dombret - John Lipsky
13-04	- The State and Outlook of the US and Chinese Economy - Japan's Abenomics and Foreign Policy	- David Hale - Hugh Patrick/ Gerald Curtis

	Title	Author
13-05	- The Creative Economy and Culture in Korea - Abenomics, Future of the Japanese Economy and the TPP	- Guy Sorman - Yukiko Fukagawa/ Jeffrey Schott
13-06	- Unified Germany in Europe: An Economic Perspective - Chinese Economic Policymaking: A Foreigners' Perspective	- Karl-Heinz Paqué - Bob Davis
13-07	- The Outlook for Japan under Abenomics and Abenationalism - After the Pax Americana (Korea-China-Japan Political and Economic Relation: Whither to?)	- David Asher - David Filling

2014

	Title	Author
14-01	U.S. and Global Economics-Poised for Better Times	- Allen Sinai
14-02	- Abe in the Driver's Seat: Where is the Road Leading? - The Secret of Germany's Performance: The Mittelstand Economy	- Gerald Curtis - Peter Friedrich
14-03	- The Eurozone Economy: Out of the Doldrums? - The Globla Economy 2014	- Karl-Heinz Paqué - Martin Feldstein
14-04	Philanthropy and Welfare	- Guy Sorman
14-05	- Global Trade Environment and the Future of the World Economy - From BRICs to America	- Roberto Azevêdo - Sung Won Sohn
14-06	- Risks and Opportunities in the Global Economic Recovery - Abe's Labor Reform and Innovative Strategies	- Charles H. Dallara - Yukiko Fukagawa
14-07	- China's Economy and Anti-Corruption Drive - US Fed's QE Ending & Asian Financial Markets - China's New Economic Strategies and the Korea-China FTA	- Bob Davis - Anoop Singh - Zhang Yunling

2015

	Title	Author
15-01	- Will the Global Economy Normalize in 2015?	- Allen Sinai
15-02	- The EU Economy in 2015: Will It Take Off? - U.S.-Korea Economic Relations: Partnership for Shared Economic Prosperity - The Hartz Labor Reforms of Germany and the Implications for Korea	- Jeroen Dijsselbloem - Mark W. Lippert - Peter Hartz
15-03	- What Makes China Grow? - What can Korea Learn from Europe's Slow Growth?	- Lawrence Lau - Guy Sorman

	Title	Author
15-04	- Global Energy and Environmental Issues and Switzerland - The Emerging New Asian Economic Disorder	- H.E. Doris Leuthard - David L. Asher
15-05	- The Chinese Economy: Transition towards the New Normal - Germany's Industry 4.0: Harnessing the Potential of Digitization	- Huang Yiping - Matthias Machnig
15-06	- Four Global Forces Changing the World - Turbulence in Emerging Markets and Impact on Korea	- Dominic Barton - Sung-won Sohn
15-07	- Observations on the Korean Economy and North Korea's Economic Potential - Perspectives on China's Economy and Economic Reform	- Thomas Byrne - Huang Haizhou

2016

	Title	Author
16-01	- The U.S. and Global Prospects and Markets in 2016: A Look Ahead	- Allen Sinai
16-02	- The Key Themes and Risks of the Global Economy in 2016 - The U.S. in the Global Economy	- Hung Tran - Anne Krueger
16-03	- The Prospects and Impact of the U.S. Election and Economy - The US and Northeast Asia in a Turbulent Time	- Martin Feldstein - Gerald Curtis
16-04	- The U.S. Presidential Election and Its Economic and Security Implications - The World Economy at a Time of Monetary Experimentation and Political Fracture - Allies in Business: The Future of the U.S.-ROK Economic Relationship	- Marcus Noland & Sung-won Sohn - Charles H. Dallara - Mark Lippert

2017

	Title	Author
17-01	- Big Changes, Big Effects - U.S. and Global Economic and Financial Prospects 2017	- Allen Sinai
17-02	- The 2017 US and Global Macroeconomic Outlook - Automation, Jobs and the Future of Work in Korea	- Martin Feldstein - Jonathan Woetzel
17-03	- Trump's US, Japan's Economy and Korea - Between Brexit and Trump: Global Challenges for the European Union	- Gerald Curtis & Hugh Paztrick - Thomas Wieser
17-04	- The Future of Work: Is This Time Different?	- Carl Benedikt Frey

	Title	Author
17-05	- The Future of Growth - The Current State of US Economy and Trump Administration's Trade Policy with Special Reference to the KORUS FTA Revision	- Simon Baptist - Sung-won Sohn & Jeffrey Schott

2018

	Title	Author
18-01	- Dr. Martin Feldstein's Analysis of the US and Global Economy - U.S. and Global Prospects Looking Ahead	- Martin Feldstein - Allen Sinai
18-02	- US Protectionism, China's Political Shift and Their Implications - Japan's Labor Reform and Future Korea-Japan Cooperation	- Kenneth Courtis - Yukiko Fukagawa
18-03	- U.S. Economic and Trade Policy for Korea and Asia - How Europeans See China, Changing World Order and Its Implications for Korea	- Charles Freeman - Guy Sorman
18-04	- Asia's New Economic Landscape: India, Japan and China - Climate, Energy and Green Tech: Transforming Our Economies	- Eisuke Sakakibara - Karsten Sach

2019

	Title	Author
19-01	- Financial Innovation, FinTech and the Future of Finance - Setting up Canada's National Pension System for Success – CPPIB's Perspectives	- Robert Merton - Suyi Kim
19-02	- Why I Remain Optimistic about China: Why China's Worst Enemy in the Short-Term Will Prove its Best Friend in the Long-Term - The World in 2019: U.S., Global Economies, Policies and Markets – Can Expansion be sustained?	- Henny Sender - Allen Sinai
19-03	- A Brief Tour of Global Near-term Risks and Long-run Concerns about the International Financial Architecture - 5 Ways the Financial System Will Fail Next Time	-Carmen Reinhart -Michael Barr
19-04	- Beyond 1980's: The New Horizon of Japan-Korea Economic Relations - Reflections on the Japanese Economy and Abenomics	-Yukiko Fukagawa -Hugh Patrick
19-05	- Financial Innovation and Asset Management Strategies in the Age of Hyper-Low Interest Rates	- Robert Merton
19-06	- Artificial Intelligence (AI) and its Impact on the Future of Economy and Society - U.S.-China, Korea-Japan Trade Disputes and the Global Trading System	- Jerome Glenn - Jeffrey Schott

		Title	Author
19-10	Oct 22	Financial Innovation and Asset Management Strategies in the Age of Hyper−Low Interest Rates	Robert Merton
19-11	Nov 19	Artificial Intelligence (AI) and its Impact on the Future of Economy and Society	Jerome Glenn

2020

		Title	Author
20-01	Jan 16	Charting 'Uncharted Waters': The U.S. and World in 2020	Allen Sinai
20-02	May 28	The 30th Anniversary of the German Reunification: Lessons and Policy Implications	Stephan Auer

2021

	Title	Author
21-01	- Geopolitical Challenges and Opportunities in East Asia Under the Biden Administration - Emerging Trends and Issues for International Capital Markets and BlackRock's ESG Strategy - 2021 Global and Asia Pacific Regional Economic Outlook - Prospects for the U.S. and Global Economies and Financial Markets in 2021	- Evans J.R. Revere - Henny Sender - Shaun Roache - Allen Sinai
21-02	- Biden Administration's Foreign Policy on Asia: Prospects for US-China Relations and Implications for Korea - The Future of International Trading System under the Biden Administration and Its Implications for Korea: Whither US Commercial Policy toward Asia?	- Victor Cha - Jeffrey J. Schott

2022

	Title	Author
22-01	- The Future of Cryptocurrency - Perspectives on ESG Investing from CPP Investments & Prospects for International Financial Markets - China's Economy at a Crossroads: Implications for US-China Relations and Korea	- Brian Brooks - Suyi Kim - David Dollar
22-02	- 2022 Prospects for Global Economy and Trade, and Implications for Korea - Geopolitical Risk Proliferation and Role of the ROK-US Alliance: Policy Implications for the New Korean administration - New Challenges for World Trade after Russia's Invasion of Ukraine	- Anne Krueger - Victor Cha - Jeffrey J. Schott

2023

	Title	Author
23-01	- Navigating the Global Multiple Economic Crises: Geopolitical and Policy Implications for Korea - US-Korea Alliance: New Challenges, New Strength - Supply Chain Crisis: Myths and Realities - Global Financial Market Turmoil Emergency Check: Asia, are we going under again?	- Charles H. Dallara - Evans J.R. Revere - Robert Dohner - Tai Hui
23-02	- The Future of US-China Decoupling Amid Weakening Chinese Economic Prospects - S.Korea diplomatic and security policy review and Implications for cooperation with US & Japan - US-China Conflict: A New Roadmap to Restoring Mutually Advantageous Relationship - 2023 Global Economic Prospects and the Challenges for Korea	- Nicholas R. Lardy - Victor Cha - Stephen Roach - Robert Subbaraman

2024

	Title	Author
24-01	- The Bitcoin Spot ETF and Its Implications for the Future of Finance - The Road Ahead: Key Global Geopolitical Challenges and Path Forward to 2024 - 2024 Global Trade and East Asia Economy Outlook: The Future of Korea-Japan Cooperation	- Brian Brooks - Gi-Wook Shin - Fukagawa Yukiko
24-02	- Geopolitical Challenges for East Asia with the 2024 US Presidential Election: Implications for S. Korea's Diplomatic and Security Policies - US Post-Election Trade Policy Outlook and Implications for China & Korea Economy	- Victor Cha - Jeffrey J. Schott

세계경제연구원 간행물

Occasional Paper Series

1993

연 번	제 목	저 자
93-01	Clintonomics and the New World Order: Implications for Korea-US Relations	C. Fred Bergsten
93-02	The Uruguay Round, NAFTA, and US-Korea Economic Relations	Jeffrey Schott

1994

연 번	제 목	저 자
94-01	21세기 준비 어떻게 할 것인가	Paul Kennedy
94-02	미국과 일본 간의 기술경쟁과 한국에 미칠 영향	Ronald A. Morse
94-03	일본경제, 무엇이 문제인가	Toyoo Gyohten
94-04	미국경제와 세계경제: 현황과 전망	Allen Sinai
94-05	국제환율제도 이대로 좋은가	John Williamson
94-06	The Promises of the WTO for the Trading Community	Arthur Dunkel

1995

연 번	제 목	저 자
95-01	멕시코 페소화 위기와 세계금융시장 동향	Charles H. Dallara
95-02	세계경제 동향과 미국경제 전망	Allen Sinai
95-03	새로운 게임, 새로운 규칙과 새로운 전략	Lester Thurow
95-04	미국 · 북한관계 전망	Robert Scalapino
95-05	미국의 동아시아 정책과 한반도	James A. Baker Ⅲ
95-06	미일 무역마찰과 한국	Anne O. Krueger
95-07	동북아경제권 개발 전망: 일본의 시각	Hisao Kanamori

1996

연 번	제 목	저 자
96-01	Trends of International Financial Market and Prospects of Global Economy in 1996	Allen Sinai
96-02	유럽연합(EU)의 앞날과 세계경제	Jørgen Ørstrøm Møller
96-03	세계경제와 OECD의 역할	Donald Johnston
96-04	동아시아 경제성장의 정치적 배경과 영향	Francis Fukuyama

연 번	제 목	저 자
96-05	국제사회에서의 한국의 새 역할	A. W. Clausen

1997

연 번	제 목	저 자
97-01	다국적기업과 동아시아 경제통합	Wendy Dobson
97-02	아태 지역에 대한 미국의 안보정책	William J. Perry
97-03	뉴질랜드의 공공부문 개혁	Donald Hunn

1998

연 번	제 목	저 자
98-01	범세계적 기업과 다자간 투자협정	Edward M. Graham
98-02	변화 속의 안정: 새로운 한미 관계의 모색	W. Anthony Lake
98-03	한국: 동북아의 새로운 협력 중심으로	Donald P. Gregg
98-04	경제적 측면에서 본 독일 통일의 교훈	Juergen B. Donges
98-05	세계화와 종족화: 20세기 말의 딜레마	Guy Sorman

1999

연 번	제 목	저 자
99-01	북한의 정치·경제 상황과 동북아 안보	Marcus Noland
99-02	엔-달러 환율과 국제금융시장	Kenneth S. Courtis
99-03	한국과 아시아 경제: 전망과 정책대응	Donald Johnston/ Hubert Neiss
99-04	미국과 일본경제의 비교평가	Hugh Patrick
99-05	세계경제: 도전과 전망	Rudiger Dornbusch

2000

연 번	제 목	저 자
00-01	한미관계: 번영과 안보의 동반자	Stephen W. Bosworth
00-02	글로벌 뉴 이코노미: 도전과 한국의 활로	양수길
00-03	금융감독의 세계적 조류	이용근
00-04	성장하는 아시아와 침체 속의 일본	Kenneth S. Courtis
00-05	세계금융체제의 미래와 우리의 대응	Morris Goldstein
00-06	시애틀 이후의 WTO와 한미FTA전망	Jeffrey Schott/ 최인범
00-07	다자간 국제경제기구의 미래와 전망	Anne O. Krueger
00-08	남북한 관계: 현황과 전망	Marcus Noland

연 번	제 목	저 자
00-09	Knowledge 시대의 외국인 직접투자 유치	Andrew Fraser
00-10	미국 新행정부 및 의회의 대외·경제정책방향	C. Fred Bergsten
00-11	한미관계: 번영과 안보의 동반자	Stephen W. Bosworth
00-12	2000년 국제금융 및 신흥시장 전망	Charles H. Dallara/ Robert Hormats
00-13	기업·금융 관계: 현황과 전망	이용근
00-14	금융세계화, 어떻게 대처하나	James P. Rooney

2001

연 번	제 목	저 자
01-01	2001년 미국, 일본경제와 아시아	Kenneth S. Courtis
01-02	부시행정부의 對韓 경제정책과 한국의 대응	Marcus Noland
01-03	3C를 극복하자	Jeffrey D. Jones
01-04	하이테크와 비즈니스, 그리고 세계경제	John Naisbitt
01-05	한국과 IMF	Stanley Fischer
01-06	한국경제의 향후 10년	Dominic Barton
01-07	세계 달러본위제도와 동아시아 환율딜레마	Ronald McKinnon
01-08	新국제질서 속의 유럽과 한국	Pierre Jacquet

2002

연 번	제 목	저 자
02-01	금융위기 再發 어떻게 막나: 칠레의 경험을 중심으로	Carlos Massad
02-02	세계경제의 기회와 위험	Martin Wolf
02-03	美·日 경제현황과 한국의 대응	Marcus Noland
02-04	미국경제와 세계경제: 회복가능성과 위험	Allen Sinai
02-05	세계화: 혜택의 원동력	Patricia Hewitt
02-06	9·11테러사태 이후의 세계질서: 문명의 충돌인가?	Francis Fukuyama
02-07	아시아지역의 통화·금융 협력	Barry Eichengreen
02-08	세계경제, 회복되나?	Kenneth S. Courtis
02-09	미국경제와 달러의 장래	Marcus Noland
02-10	도하라운드: 문제점과 전망	Jagdish Bhagwati
02-11	2003 한국경제와 세계경제 전망	Paul F. Gruenwald
02-12	미국경제 현황과 세계경제의 앞날	John B. Taylor
02-13	9·11사태와 미국의 한반도정책	Thomas C. Hubbard
02-14	미국 경제, 달러 및 대외통상정책 방향	C. Fred Bergsten
02-15	미국의 IT산업 관련 정책과 한국	Peter F. Cowhey

2003

연 번	제 목	저 자
03-01	이라크전 이후의 미국경제와 세계경제	Allen Sinai
03-02	OECD가 본 한국경제	Donald Johnston
03-03	아태 지역에서의 미국의 새 역할	Charles Morrison
03-04	세계경제 전망과 부시행정부의 경기부양책	Phil Gramm
03-05	침체된 독일·유럽 경제가 주는 정책적 교훈과 시사	Hans Tietmeyer
03-06	동아시아 금융협력과 한국	Eisuke Sakakibara
03-07	세계환율체제 개편과 동아시아 경제	John Williamson

2004

연 번	제 목	저 자
04-01	2004 미국경제와 세계경제 전망	Allen Sinai
04-02	김정일 이후의 한반도	Marcus Noland
04-03	미국 대통령 선거와 韓·美·日관계	Hugh Patrick/ Gerald Curtis
04-04	중국경제의 부상과 동북아 지역경제	Zhang Yunling
04-05	아시아 화폐단일화, 가능한가?	Robert Mundell
04-06	외국기업인의 눈에 비친 한국경제	William C. Oberlin

2005

연 번	제 목	저 자
05-01	대통령선거 이후의 미국 통상정책, 어떻게 되나	Peter F. Cowhey
05-02	아시아 경제·무역환경, 어떻게 전개되나?	Dominic Barton
05-03	제2기 부시 행정부의 경제정책과 세계경제 및 시장 전망	Allen Sinai
05-04	일본의 시각에서 본 한국경제의 활로	Yukiko Fukagawa
05-05	세계경제, 무엇이 문제인가	Barry Eichengreen
05-06	세계 속의 한국경제: 역할과 전망	Anne O. Krueger
05-07	중국과 인도가 세계경제에 미치는 영향	Wendy Dobson
05-08	동아시아와 아태지역 경제통합	Robert Scollay
05-09	국제신용평가기관이 보는 한국	Thomas Byrne

2006

연 번	제 목	저 자
06-01	고유가와 세계경제의 앞날	Philip K. Verleger
06-02	2006년 미국경제/세계경제와 금융시장 전망	Allen Sinai

연 번	제 목	저 자
06-03	한미FTA: 지속성장의 활로	Alexander Vershbow
06-04	일본의 대외경제정책과 한일 FTA	Oshima Shotaro
06-05	일본경제 회생과 한국경제	Yukiko Fukagawa
06-06	세계 M&A시장 현황과 전망: 우리의 대응	Robert F. Bruner
06-07	세계인이 보는 한국경제는?	Charles H. Dallara
06-08	아시아 공통통화와 아시아 경제통합	Eisuke Sakakibara
06-09	미국의 힘은 얼마나 강하며, 중국의 부상은 어떻게 보아야 하는가?	Paul Kennedy/ Bernard Gordon
06-10	- 20년 후의 중국, 어떤 모습일까? - 세계 IT 리더십 경쟁: 승자와 패자	- Richard N. Cooper - George Scalise

2007

연 번	제 목	저 자
07-01	한미관계: 새로운 동반자 시대를 지향하며	Edwin J. Feulner
07-02	통일 이후 독일: 경제침체의 교훈	Juergen B. Donges
07-03	2007년 세계경제와 금융시장의 지각변동	Allen Sinai
07-04	급변하는 세계경제환경, 어떻게 대처해야 하나	Angel Gurría
07-05	동아시아 FTA 가능한가?: 중국의 시각	Zhang Yunling
07-06	구조적 변화 맞고 있는 세계석유시장과 한국	Fereidun Fesharaki
07-07	변모하는 세계경제와 한국	Anne O. Krueger
07-08	되살아나는 일본경제: 전망과 과제	Yukiko Fukagawa
07-09	디지털 네트워크 경제와 글로벌 기업 전략	Ben Verwaayen
07-10	한미FTA: 미국의 시각	Jeffrey Schott
07-11	한미FTA와 한국경제의 미래	Barry Eichengreen
07-12	- 동아시아 경제통합, 어떻게 보나 - 한국경제 및 동아시아경제 전망	- David Hale - Jerald Schiff
07-13	- 21세기는 여전히 미국의 세기가 될 것인가? - 인도경제 전망과 한국 기업	- Guy Sorman - Tarun Das

2008

연 번	제 목	저 자
08-01	국가 미래를 위한 한국의 세계화 전략	Anne O. Krueger
08-02	2008년 미국경제와 세계금융시장 동향	Allen Sinai
08-03	유럽의 경제침체: 우리에게 주는 시사점	Guy Sorman
08-04	차기 미국 대통령이 풀어야할 세계적 도전	James A. Baker III
08-05	일본 자본시장의 현재와 전망	Atsushi Saito

연 번	제 목	저 자
08-06	대선 이후 미국의 정치·경제, 어떻게 전개되나?	Phil Gramm
08-07	세계 및 아시아 경제·금융 전망	Charles H. Dallara
08-08	한국경제의 경쟁력 강화, 어떻게 하나?	Guy Sorman
08-09	- 국부펀드: 인식과 현실 - 긴장 속의 세계금융시장, 어떻게 되나?	- Robert C. Pozen - Jeffrey R. Shafer

2009

연 번	제 목	저 자
09-01	2009년 한국경제와 세계 및 아시아 경제 전망	Subir Lall
09-02	혼란과 전환기의 경쟁력 강화: 과제와 전망	Deborah Wince-Smith
09-03	위기 속의 미국 및 세계 경제와 금융: 전망과 정책대응	Allen Sinai
09-04	미국 오바마 행정부의 통상정책	Jeffrey Schott
09-05	하강하는 세계경제와 케인지언 정책 처방의 실효성	Justin Yifu Lin
09-06	- 세계금융위기가 개도국에 미치는 여파와 대응 - 최근 세계경제위기의 교훈과 전망	- Danny Leipziger - Anne O. Krueger
09-07	- 미국 오바마 행정부의 경제 및 대외정책, 어떻게 되나? - 한미 경제 파트너십: 세계적 위기에 어떻게 협력할 것인가	- Guy Sorman - Jeffrey Schott

2010

연 번	제 목	저 자
10-01	새로운 세계질서 속에 변화하는 EU: 한국의 기회는?	Jean-Pierre Lehmann
10-02	위기 이후 미국 및 세계경제 전망, 그리고 유산과 정책 과제	Allen Sinai
10-03	세계경제, 어떻게 볼 것인가?: 진단과 전망	Anne O. Krueger
10-04	- 세계화 파고 속의 한국과 일본경제: 도전과 전망 - 중국 경제의 虛와 實	- Yukiko Fukagawa - Danny Leipziger
10-05	- 신흥국 자본시장과 뉴 프런티어 - 세계경제와 아시아의 역할	- Mark Mobius - Dominique Strauss-Kahn
10-06	세계경제의 재균형	Paul A. Volcker

2011

연 번	제 목	저 자
11-01	위기 이후의 세계경제와 한국경제: 2011년 및 2012년 전망	Allen Sinai
11-02	원자력 발전의 안전성과 경제성: 한국의 선택은?	장순흥
11-03	중국 경제의 재(再)균형	Yu Yongding
11-04	세계금융질서의 개편: 아시아의 시각	세계경제연구원
11-05	- 아시아 경제의 발전전망과 도전과제 - 유럽의 국가채무위기: 평가와 전망	- Haruhiko Kuroda - Richard N. Cooper
11-06	- 기로에 선 세계화와 다자주의, 그리고 G-20 - 북한의 시장과 경제, 그리고 정치적 안정성, 어떻게 변화하고 있나?	- Danny Leipziger - Marcus Noland

2012

연 번	제 목	저 자
12-01	혼돈 속의 세계경제와 금융시장: 분석과 2012년 전망	Allen Sinai
12-02	- 카이스트의 혁신 - 유로위기 해결책은 없나	- 서남표 - Hans Martens
12-03	- 2012년 미국의 대선과 향후 아태정책 전망 - 세계경제 및 금융시장 현황 - 그래도 세계경제의 미래는 밝다	- Charles Morrison - Charles H. Dallara - Guy Sorman
12-04	- FTA와 아태지역 통합 그리고 한국 - 유로위기 언제 끝나나?	- Peter A. Petri - Nicolas Véron
12-05	- 중국의 새 리더십과 경제정책 - 국제통상질서의 현황과 WTO의 미래	- Andrew Sheng - Jean-Pierre Lehmann

2013

연 번	제 목	저 자
13-01	2013년 세계경제와 미국경제 전망	Allen Sinai
13-02	유로존, 올해는 위기에서 벗어날 수 있나?	Guntram B. Wolff
13-03	- 유럽국채위기: 과제와 해결책 - 세계경제, 언제 회복되나?	- Andreas Dombret - John Lipsky
13-04	- 미국과 중국경제 현황과 전망 - 일본의 아베노믹스와 외교정책	- David Hale - Hugh Patrick/Gerald Curtis
13-05	- 한국의 창조경제와 문화 - 아베노믹스와 일본 경제의 미래, 그리고 TPP	- Guy Sorman - Yukiko Fukagawa/ Jeffrey Schott
13-06	- 통일 독일의 경제·정치적 위상: 한국에 대한 시사점 - 외국인이 바라본 중국의 경제정책	- Karl-Heinz Paqué - Bob Davis

2014

연 번	제 목	저 자
14-01	2014년 세계경제, 나아질 것인가?	Allen Sinai
14-02	- 아베정권은 어디로 가고 있나? - 중견기업: 순항하는 독일경제의 비결	- Gerald Curtis - Peter Friedrich
14-03	- 유럽경제, 살아날 것인가? - 2014년 세계 경제의 향방은?	- Karl-Heinz Paqué - Martin Feldstein
14-04	복지향상과 기부문화	Guy Sorman
14-05	- 세계무역 환경과 세계경제의 미래 - 브릭스(BRICs)에서 미국으로	- Roberto Azevêdo - Sung Won Sohn
14-06	- 세계경제 회복, 위기인가 기회인가 - 아베 정권의 노동개혁과 혁신전략은 성공할 것인가	- Charles H. Dallara - Yukiko Fukagawa
14-07	- 중국경제 현황과 시진핑의 반부패운동 - 다가올 미 연준의 QE종료가 아시아 금융시장에 미칠 영향 - 중국의 신경제 전략과 한-중 FTA	- Bob Davis - Anoop Singh - Zhang Yunling

2015

연 번	제 목	저 자
15-01	2015년 세계경제, 정상화될 것인가	Allen Sinai
15-02	- 2015년 유럽경제, 회복될 것인가? - 공동 번영을 위한 한미 경제 파트너십 - 독일 하르츠 노동개혁과 한국에 대한 시사점	- Jeroen Dijsselbloem - Mark W. Lippert - Peter Hartz
15-03	- 중국 경제의 앞날을 내다보며 - 유럽의 저성장에서 우리는 무엇을 배워야 하는가?	- Lawrence Lau - Guy Sorman
15-04	- 글로벌 에너지(중점)환경 이슈와 스위스의 경험 - 혼돈의 아시아 경제, 어디로 가는가	- H.E. Doris Leuthard - David L. Asher
15-05	- 중국 경제의 신창타이(新常態)는 무엇인가 - 디지털화를 활용한 독일의 산업혁명 4.0	- Huang Yiping - Matthias Machnig
15-06	- 세상을 바꾸는 네 가지 글로벌 흐름 - 격변하는 신흥시장과 한국에 미칠 영향	- Dominic Barton - Sung-won Sohn
15-07	- 내가 본 한국, 한국 경제, 그리고 북한 경제의 잠재력 - 중국의 경제개혁과 향후 전망	- Thomas Byrne - Huang Haizhou

2016

연 번	제 목	저 자
16-01	2016년 세계경제 및 금융시장 전망	- Allen Sinai
16-02	- 2016년 세계 경제의 주요 이슈와 리스크 - 미국의 경제·정치 상황이 세계 경제에 미치는 영향	- Hung Tran - Anne Krueger
16-03	- 미국 경제와 대선이 세계 경제에 미칠 영향 - 미국 대통령 선거가 동북아에 미칠 지정학적 영향과 전망	- Martin Feldstein - Gerald Curtis

연 번	제 목	저 자
16-04	- 미국 새 행정부의 경제와 안보 정책 - 통화정책 실험과 정치 분열기의 세계 경제 - 한미 경제 협력: 현황과 전망	- Marcus Noland & Sung-won Sohn - Charles H. Dallara - Mark Lippert

2017

연 번	제 목	저 자
17-01	- 대변혁 속의 2017 - 미국과 세계 경제 금융 전망	- Allen Sinai
17-02	- 미국 신정부의 경제정책과 2017년 미국 및 세계 경제 전망 - 4차 산업혁명 시대 자동화, 일자리, 그리고 직업의 미래	- Martin Feldstein - Jonathan Woetzel
17-03	- 트럼프의 미국, 일본 경제 그리고 한국 - 브렉시트와 미국의 트럼프 대통령: 유럽의 도전	- Gerald Curtis & Hugh Patrick - Thomas Wieser
17-04	- 직업의 미래 - 이번엔 다른가	- Carl Benedikt Frey
17-05	- 세계경제 성장 전망과 기술의 역할 - 미국경제 현황과 트럼프 행정부의 통상정책 및 한미 FTA 개정	- Simon Baptist - Sung-won Sohn &Jeffrey Schott

2018

연 번	제 목	저 자
18-01	- 펠드스타인 교수가 진단하는 미국과 세계경제 - 2018년 미국과 세계 경제·금융 전망	- Martin Feldstein - Allen Sinai
18-02	- 미국 보호주의와 중국 정치체제 변화의 함의 - 일본 노동개혁과 한일 협력의 미래	- Kenneth Courtis - Yukiko Fukagawa
18-03	- 트럼프 행정부의 한국 및 대아시아 무역·경제 정책 - 유럽이 보는 시진핑 체제하의 중국과 세계 질서	- Charles Freeman - Guy Sorman
18-04	- 새로운 아시아 경제 지평: 일본, 중국 그리고 인도 - 독일의 기후변화, 에너지 및 녹색기술 정책 경험과 한국에 대한 시사점	- Eisuke Sakakibara - Karsten Sach

2019

연 번	제 목	저 자
19-01	- 금융혁신, 핀테크 그리고 금융의 미래 - 캐나다 국민연금 시스템의 성공과 CPPIB	- Robert Merton - Suyi Kim
19-02	- 내가 중국 경제를 여전히 낙관하는 이유: 왜 중국의 단기적 악재가 장기적 호재일까 - 2019년 세계 경제 및 금융 전망 - 과연 경기 확장세는 지속될 것인가?	- Henny Sender - Allen Sinai

연 번	제 목	저 자
19-03	국제금융체제의 단기 리스크와 구조적 문제 향후 금융시스템 실패의 5가지 시나리오	-Carmen Reinhart -Michael Barr
19-04	한 · 일 무역갈등을 넘어서: 양국 경제관계의 새로운 지평 휴 패트릭 교수가 본 일본경제와 아베노믹스	-Yukiko Fukagawa -Hugh Patrick
19-05	초저금리 시대의 금융 혁신과 자산운용 전략	-Robert Merton
19-06	인공지능(AI)이 만드는 경제 · 사회의 미래 미 · 중, 한 · 일 무역분쟁과 세계무역체제	- Jerome Glenn - Jeffrey Schott

2020

연 번	제 목	저 자
20-01	2020년 미국 및 세계 경제 전망: '미지의 바다' 항해도 그리기 -10개의 메시지와 코로나바이러스 충격	- Allen Sinai
20-02	독일 통일 30년의 경험: 교훈과 정책적 시사점	- Stephan Auer

2021

연 번	제 목	저 자
21-01	- 美 바이든 행정부 출범과 동아시아의 지정학적 도전 및 기회	- Evans J.R. Revere
	- 국제금융시장 현황 및 핵심 이슈와 블랙록 ESG투자 전략	- Henny Sender
	- 2021 글로벌 경제 전망: 중국 · 일본 · 한국, 아시아 경제의 향방	- Shaun Roache
	- 2021년 미국 및 세계 경제 예측과 금융시장 전망	- Allen Sinai
21-02	- 바이든 행정부의 아시아 외교정책: 미 · 중 관계 전망과 한국에 대한 시사점	- Victor Cha
	- 바이든 행정부 출범과 국제통상체제의 미래: 미국의 對아시아 통상전략 향방 및 한국에의 시사점	- Jeffrey J. Schott

2022

연 번	제 목	저 자
22-01	- 가상화폐의 미래	- Brian Brooks
	- 캐나다 연기금(CPP)의 ESG 투자 전략과 국제금융시장 전망	- Suyi Kim
	- 전환점에 선 중국 경제: 美 中 역학관계와 한국에의 시사점	- David Dollar
22-02	- 2022년 글로벌 경제 및 무역 전망: 한국에의 정책적 시사점	- Anne Krueger
	- 지정학적 리스크 확산과 한미동맹의 역할: 新 정부 외교 안보 전략 시사점	- Victor Cha
	- 러시아의 우크라이나 침공 이후 세계 무역의 새로운 도전	- Jeffrey J. Schott

2023

연 번	제 목	저 자
23-01	- 글로벌 복합 경제 위기 진단: 한국 경제에의 지정학적 및 정책적 시사점 - 한미동맹의 미래: 새로운 도전, 새로운 기회 - 글로벌 공급망 이슈 진단과 세계 경제안보 전망 - 국제 금융시장 긴급진단 웨비나: 달러 초강세 속 亞 외환위기 재발 위험 진단	- Charles H. Dallara - Evans J.R. Revere - Robert Dohner - Tai Hui
23-02	- 중국경제 둔화 전망과 미중 디커플링의 전략적 함의 - 尹정부 1년 외교안보정책 리뷰 및 한미일 공조를 위한 제언 - 美中 패권 갈등: 互惠 관계 회복을 위한 새로운 로드맵 - 2023년 세계경제 전망과 한국경제의 도전	- Nicholas R. Lardy - Victor Cha - Stephen Roach - Robert Subbaraman

2024

연 번	제 목	저 자
24-01	- 비트코인 현물 ETF 등장: 금융투자 게임체인저 되나 - 글로벌 지정학 위기 진단과 2024년 전망 및 시사점 - 2024년 글로벌 무역과 동아시아 경제 전망: 한일 협력의 미래	- Brian Brooks - Gi-Wook Shin - Fukagawa Yukiko
24-02	- 2024년 미국 대선과 동북아 지정학적 리스크: 한국의 외교안보전략 시사점 - 미국 대선 이후 무역정책 변화와 중국 및 한국 경제에 미치는 영향 분석	- Victor Cha - Jeffrey J. Schott